PREPPER'S GUIDE TO

SURVIVING NATURAL DISASTERS

JAMES D. NOWKA

Published by

Living Ready, an imprint of F+W Media, Inc.
700 East State Street • Iola, WI 54990-0001
715-445-2214 • 888-457-2873
www.livingreadyonline.com

Other fine Living Ready books are available from
your local bookstore and online suppliers.
Visit our website at www.livingreadyonline.com

ISBN-13: 978-1-4402-3566-5
ISBN-10: 1-4402-3566-X

Designed by Dave Hauser
Edited by Jared Blohm

Printed in USA

DEDICATION

I would like to dedicate this book
to the two Depression kids —
my mom and dad — who taught
me the importance of self-reliance,
and my wife, who has stood
beside me in person or in
spirit on every adventure.

CONTENTS

INTRODUCTION

Modern convenience affords our society so much more than earlier generations of Americans could've ever wished for or considered. Our forefathers, though, had a few important things of their own that have become rare in this day and age. The skills, attitude and drive they needed to simply get through their everyday challenges appear to be things that most have just let slip away.

Life is easier now. Still, I've come to wonder how much all of our modern conveniences really offer if the principles of self-reliance were handed away in trade-off. It seems so many people today lack even the basic abilities that would become necessary to ensure personal safety and survival should an emergency situation strike.

In some ways, this book is a textbook. In others, it's an instructional manual. At its heart, it's a guide on exercising common sense. I hope the following pages might bring even a few to recognize that the hard work and virtues of self-reliance exercised generations ago are just as important today as they always were.

I've worked in many different roles, traveled the world and I've seen tragedy in a variety of scales. Disasters, whether they're isolated situations or major news events, happen frequently enough that everyone should take notice. Spending some time and thought, learning some new skills and assembling the proper gear could go a long way toward soothing the sting should an emergency touch your family.

It's a matter of developing the right mindset and approaching life from a position of vigilance. It's a matter of keeping one step ahead of our many risk factors. This very moment is the best time to get started. It's far too late to entertain that very first thought of survival when a true threat is pounding at the front door.

The potential for devastation isn't an enjoyable topic for anyone to think about. It isn't difficult to understand how so many people have settled into attitudes of complacency. It's a tremendous time marked with new and unbelievable tools. Most people have access to 911 emergency services from right inside their pockets by virtue of their cellphones. Oftentimes, those same phones can also email, text, surf the internet and call up the latest news and weather reports. Many people have the ability to hit a button in their cars and quickly call on an ambulance at the first sign of trouble.

It's a double-edged sword. So many people today have false senses of security bolstered by all of their conveniences. Many

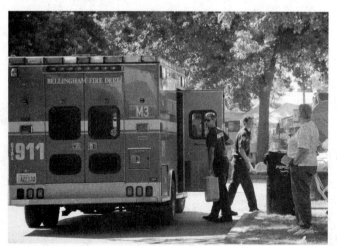

In a disaster situation, there's no guarantee 911 emergency services will be able to help you in a timely fashion. In some cases, they might not be able to help you at all.

take great and undue comfort knowing their credit cards are at easy reach. However, our phones or the plastic in our wallets would not come close to foolproof in the midst of a disaster or in its aftermath. Like the men and women of even just a generation or two earlier, we still truly need the know-how and ingenuity to be able to rely only on ourselves should any number of difficult situations require.

My own efforts toward self-reliance and dedication to planning began early with everything I learned from my dad. He was born in 1927. Through his first 20 or so years, he only knew life through the lens of the Great Depression. It wasn't until his stint was up in the Marines after World War II that he learned what real prosperity was. My dad carried away some good lessons from his younger days in that terrible economic time and put them to use for the remainder of his years. His frugal sense taught me a few things. Although my parents did well for themselves, they were never big spenders. They saved for the rainy days. They got the most from everything they had.

Today, most would rather not bother with the broken. It's a disposable society in which people expect their things to work and simply toss them aside when the first hints of problems emerge. If an item is important enough,

they will send it out for repair. My dad would certainly buy something new when the situation required, but he'd never

Credit cards are of little help when stores are without power following a disaster. It's best to keep a reserve of cash on hand for emergencies.

put the old one out to the trash bin. After all, that old piece was still good for parts. He didn't call on someone else to fix his problems because he knew he could just as easily do it himself.

It was an important lesson in taking ownership that I took to heart. Too few today are willing to put forth even a small bit of time or effort toward reaching their own solutions. It usually takes just a phone call and a little bit of cash to pass that job on to someone else. After an emergency, you might very well find there isn't a person out there available to pick up the telephone.

Many in the modern era would be lost without the ability to lean on another. It is a bit scary that so many today stand so far from the spirit exhibited by my dad's generation. It's amazing that such a dramatic shift in abilities and attitudes happened in such a short period of time.

Survival planning is an extension of that earlier ethic. It's a matter of accounting for risks, considering needs and having contingencies at the ready should a time come when you can only depend on yourself, your friends and your family. It's been said that "ignorance is bliss," and I think that best describes the approach most have taken toward preparedness. Many would rather not entertain the thought of a survival situation, and I've gotten the sense that some view preparation as a practice in pessimism.

I certainly wouldn't consider myself among those who see the cup half empty — quite the contrary. I've always been a troubleshooter, and that's what really set the foundation for all of my own efforts. I've long had a particular knack for identifying problems and, more importantly, reaching workable solutions.

Comfort and even survival in the aftermath of a disaster could hinge on the solutions you assemble long in advance. Preparing for the worst and expecting it are two very different mindsets. I'm not looking over my shoulder expecting to find trouble, but if trouble happened to find me, I know I'd be ready.

You shouldn't lose sight that trouble is most certainly out there. My extensive travel and first-hand glances in the aftermath of some of the world's most devastating natural disasters only strengthened my beliefs on the value of proper planning. Efforts made amid the everyday calm are the only way to adequately ensure the very staples of survival — namely shelter, water and food — are ready and quickly available when disaster ushers chaos into a community.

Along my path, I've worked part-time as a firefighter and as a law enforcement officer. I'm a diver with experience in body recovery. Contract work took me across the country and around the globe. I did electronic surveillance for the Army in Iraq and worked with Special Forces as an agricultural adviser in Afghanistan. I've taken my skills to tattered regions in the aftermath of four hurricanes. Those efforts made it crystal clear that bad things happen. They happen to good people and Mother Nature doesn't stop to think about who is best or least prepared before she flexes her destructive muscles.

I've worked in the midst of worst-case scenarios. It was humbling and inspiring to watch the human spirit at work in the aftermath of tragedy. Often, it was difficult.

In 2010, I looked on as survivors of Haiti's 7.0-magnitude earthquake did their best to prop up rubble in attempts to form any semblance of suitable shelter. Survivors bartered among each other for supplies. People worked together. Some walked mile after long mile just to fill up jugs of water amid constant, unrelenting clouds of dust.

They did the best they could as most mourned their many loved ones lost to the destruction. The people of most countries rely on professionals to handle body recovery efforts. Families there dug through the rubble with their own bare hands to free the bodies of friends and family members who didn't make it. Words can't adequately describe the depth of the destruction or the heartache.

Relief work on the home front brought me to the aftermaths of hurricanes Rita, Ike and Gustav. Hurricane Ike made landfall within weeks of Gustav and our crew went from one recovery operation to the second. It's always been amazing to see the dedication and efforts of those tirelessly working to bring life back normal after chaos. Our group went to Texas in Ike's wake, and in only two days, built a camp that housed and fed 2,000 workers.

In 2005, I provided security for fellow workers in New Orleans after Hurricane Katrina's unmerciful wrath and had another surreal

view at just how unforgiving the elements of our world can be. There, I encountered people who did their best to gather everything they needed only to

The author has worked in the aftermath of some of the world's most devastating natural disasters. That experience has only strengthened his resolve to make sure his family is prepared if a disaster strikes.

be stifled by growing flood waters. People were quickly confronted by choices of property or survival. It was jarring to see those who waded through water with loaded-up storage tubs floating aside them knowing the contents made up everything they had left in the world.

It was another experience that made it clear just how much people stand to gain with some dedication to planning and adequate respect for nature's power. Though I couldn't help but feel a certain degree of sympathy, it's still difficult to shake the fact that New Orleans had adequate warning. So many people, regardless of their situations, could have done so much better for themselves with appropriate forethought and effort. It all comes back to planning.

Risks exist wherever you call home. Some live near industrial areas that could present the chance of chemical spills. Large stretches of the country are at significant risk for tornadoes. It isn't a threat to ignore when considering the numbers. The United States experiences more tornadoes than any other country on the planet and averages more than 1,000 each year.

People across the country live in floodplains. In the United States, flooding takes lives and causes billions of dollars in damages annually. A 30-year average from 1981 through 2010 attributed $7.82 billion in damages to flooding and 91 deaths each year.

Others live in regions prone to wildfires. The fires burned through an average of 6.5 million acres of land across the country annually from 2001 through 2010. Many make their homes near fault lines and live with the potential for earthquakes.

It's easier for many to consider catastrophe impersonally and from afar. You should take some time to envision yourself and your family directly in the shoes of those wondering what they'll do next after a disaster took everything. Families who survive destructive tornadoes, for instance, not only deal with home loss but often the reality that their prized possessions are lost forever. It isn't uncommon for tornadoes to pick up goods and toss them across several counties.

Wildfires rapidly spread through woodland areas throughout many areas of the United States every year. Families in those affected zones often get no more than an hour's notice when it's time to evacuate. It's tough to imagine having such a tight window to rush through the home, decide what to take and what pieces of a hard-earned livelihood the family would have to let go to ruin.

In a typical and even destructive house fire, many families will return and find some degree of hope in the form of a few salvageable items. They might collect some heirlooms or a few pieces of furniture from the rubble. In a wildfire situation, everything is very literally gone. Every picture, every book and every piece of clothing left behind is often turned to ash.

You shouldn't take your life or any bit of your prosperity for granted. I've looked into the eyes of those who survived catastrophic loss. Dazed and confused would be the best description I can offer for the expressions on faces when people settle into the realization they've just lost it all.

You can't stop disaster, but you can do your best to mitigate the level of harm it brings. Preparedness is a way of life that recognizes that bad things do happen. It's a pursuit in developing the flexibility necessary to tackle unforeseen challenges as they come to bear.

Every day brings some degree of uncertainty. My overall career arc beyond rescue operations, security and emergency services speaks loudly to the truth that none of us can possibly know what's around the next corner. The only real threads tying together my varied experiences have been a continual exercise of flexibility and a strong reliance on problem solving.

As a kid, all I ever wanted was to become a dairy farmer, and after college, I fulfilled that dream. High interest rates on my property combined with low commodity prices eventually forced our difficult decision to move on. From there, I obtained my necessary licenses, bought a tugboat and ran a successful operation for a few years. Later, I became a storeowner and, as part of that business, worked out solutions for boaters who ran into troubles on Lake Michigan. That career was pulled from beneath our family when the owner of my leased building sold it off to the city for demolition.

Fortunately, I discovered the Internet. In 1998, I bought the website knifeforums.com and built it into a successful online operation that's become a strong source of news, opinion and community for knife collectors and enthusiasts. Today, it's an active and multi-faceted site that frequently touches on survival and preparedness issues. I've learned from my visitors, and my visitors have learned from each other. I'm proud of what it's become.

The author has performed electronic surveillance for the Army in Iraq and worked with Special Forces as an agricultural adviser in Afghanistan.

Life has been a great and wild ride, and the experiences along the way continually brought clearer focus to one key nugget of truth. A life well lived is a matter of anticipating problems, meeting challenges when they rise and coming out stronger on the other side. The further ahead you can set your sights, the better off you'll be.

Preparation is empowerment. There's a certain strength that comes in knowing that while a disaster would test your emotions, you could get by, live safely and assure the wellbeing of your family. The well prepared are also able to provide for some level of comfort.

Consider this book as a road map to some peace of mind and take the initial steps down that path. Those who dismiss the value of preparedness stand to someday become an example of another oft spoken phrase: "Hindsight is 20-20." Disasters happen.

Disasters have been and will always be a regular part of life on this planet. It's a roll of the dice to ignore the dangers. The floods, tornadoes, hurricanes or fires harming those across the country or halfway around the world today could just as easily harm your own neighborhood come tomorrow.

Preparation starts easily enough with some good, honest thinking. A minimal plan would at least need to account for survival basics. You wouldn't make it long without food, water and appropriate shelter. Those new to readiness planning should apply those needs to the real-life possibilities that come with where and how your families live. It's at that point you can start to forge some solutions.

Those on the front end of their preparations should consider whether the pantry is appropriately stocked. You should think about how to account for water needs if an emergency broke off the connection to the well or municipal supply. Those living way up in the northernmost regions of the country should have some plans for keeping warm should the furnace go out. By the same reasoning, those living in hurricane zones should have their shutters ready to go.

Watching the human spirit at work in the aftermath of tragedy, like the Haiti earthquake in 2010, has humbled and inspired the author.

Regardless of where you are living, it's a matter of breaking down and solving the many smaller challenges that any disaster and its aftermath could present to your family. The well prepared will have enough knowledge in first aid to provide immediate care to the injured should a disaster slow the response times of paramedics. A diligent prepper will have appropriate gear ready to go should an emergency require a quick getaway.

It's not only a matter of developing plans but also working with them. Families should practice, become familiar and develop a certain comfort in the solutions devised for each of your reasonable risks. It's an ongoing process. It's a matter of keeping the mind focused on safety. The very first step is getting past one dangerous notion held by far too many. No one should ever think, "It'll never happen to me."

The potential for tough times

nudges right up to individual households on a frequent basis. Anyone who's spent any time in front of the television has watched on when those colorful weather graphics cover up half of the screen as severe storms approach and move through his or her region. People run into hard times every day, and often, disaster situations aren't so deadly or widespread as to draw the entire nation's sustained attention.

Any number of situations could be rife with difficulties for those who didn't put together a winning game plan. At my home in northern Michigan, for instance, it's fairly common to see a blizzard or two every winter. Each carries the risk of interrupting power and blocking off our streets. It's a toss of the coin as to whether power will come back quickly or whether the trucks can make quick, decent headway on a foot or more of snow. Some might

The author sits on cases of Redi-Wash Self Heating Bathing Cloths in the Port-au-Prince Airport in Haiti following the 2010 earthquake. "These made us feel civil," he said.

have reason for worry. I'm comfortable because I can confidently say I'm equipped for the worst any of those storms could bring.

On the other end of the scale, the frequency of major disasters should be enough to give anyone pause. Hardships hit the headlines every single year. A year-by-year glance highlighting some of Mother Nature's recent havoc on the United States says an awful lot more than any survivalist could on the importance of well-crafted plans.

In 2009, Californians suffered a series of wildfires, including Los Angeles' Station fire that burned through more than 160,000 acres and destroyed 209 structures. Haiti's 2010 earthquake that killed more than 300,000 was the capstone of a tumultuous year on a global scale. Areas of the United States also encountered some substantial destruction that year. In 2010, middle Tennessee and western Kentucky sustained what were called "1,000-year floods" that caused more than $2 billion in damages.

In 2011, a monstrous tornado tore through Joplin, Mo., leaving 158 dead and more than 1,000 injured. In 2012, wildfires in Colorado destroyed homes by the hundreds and required thousands of people to evacuate. Hurricane Isaac flooded out homes and forced evacuations months later. Hurricane Sandy developed into the biggest Atlantic hurricane in history. Her wind speeds fell below hurricane levels before she slammed to shore in late October. The super storm nonetheless battered the East Coast, took lives and left billions in damages.

That's the reality. Disasters change lives and frequently so. They can't be ignored. Those who hold undue levels of confidence in modern improvements are setting themselves up for rude awakenings should they find themselves in the path of nature's forces.

As some take too much comfort in their personal technologies, others place too much faith in an admittedly strong emergency warning infrastructure. All are fortunate to live at a time in which notice of potentially dangerous situations has never been better. In addition to the traditional, overhead sirens, people have instant news alerts and occasional television overrides and auto-dialed telephone messages. The disasters above, however, illustrate that notice alone isn't sufficient to assure safety.

Preparing can provide some assurances. You would know there's enough to eat and a means to stay warm and dry. The idea of taking action today for the sake of tomorrow isn't a new concept.

It is a bit puzzling as to why survival preparation is so foreign to so many, when most prepare for life's big risks in other fashions. Most carry homeowner's insurance and pay the premiums without any expectation that a fire would gut the house. Every driver ponies up for car insurance with full confidence he or she will arrive at each and every destination without a scratch or dent.

In that regard, most people are pretty good at preparing when it comes to taking care of their stuff. Survival preparation is a form of insurance that takes more thought and effort. It isn't as simple as writing a check, though it accounts for the very most important matters of life — the people you love and the very skin you're in.

Certainly, people can and have made it through devastating circumstances without having the right contingencies in place. The question falls as to whether you are OK with the prospect of suffering more than necessary. The unprepared, whether it's after a tornado or even a three-day power outage, could have it easier. It's simply a matter of developing the right knowledge and storing some supplies away. It really is just a matter of common sense.

Some might hold a view of survival planning as the pursuit of those who worry too much. It's easy to understand. Preparing is frequently portrayed in the media through the eyes of those who are convinced that government collapse, mass-scale terrorism or some other world-changing event is on its way.

Preparedness isn't about doomsday. It's about

Consider this book a guide, much like a GPS or compass.

every day. It's about the neighborhood that's regrouping after the severe thunderstorm and the small town that's reeling after the tornado. Throughout the country, people are going to find themselves in untenable positions every day of the week.

Preparedness, rather, is a matter of reclaiming the all-American, get-it-done attitude. Going back to the beginnings, our forefathers came from overseas and literally hacked a life out of the forests. There wasn't an ambulance to call or a store to visit.

We're in an unprecedented time, and it isn't always for the better. Some today wouldn't attempt to change a tire should they encounter a flat while traveling down the highway. You don't have to turn back the clock or eschew modern convenience to recognize there's a better way to live than in complete reliance on others.

Preparedness builds little by little. New thoughts and skills give way to the next. Yesterday's purchase and today's practice means the plan for tomorrow is that much stronger.

It brings back another thought about life growing up. When I was a kid, my parents didn't have a credit card to reach for when the time came for that bigger purchase or longer term project. It always started with an envelope and the few dollars they had in their pockets.

They'd add to the envelope whenever and however they could, and its contents weren't touched until enough money was in there to pay for that need. Few operate that way anymore, and in a sense, preparation is the same type of practice. Preppers put a few things away and gain a few new skills. The envelope gets thicker and it's there to open when the emergency calls.

Adding to the envelope means developing an understanding of long-term food planning and means of securing safe drinking water. Plans build through basic first aid skills, personal protection efforts and having the know-how to assure the family would have safe and comfortable shelter after a disaster. Many of those lessons were just every day matters of life not so long ago.

It's called survival preparation, but comfort preparation would often be an accurate descriptor. Some plan more deeply than others, and basic survival needs provide the only rules. It's a matter of considering how much the family is reasonably willing to endure.

It's a tough world out there. Those who walk through it blindly and make it through unscathed are extremely lucky people. Preparing is holding yourself and your family in high regard from a position of healthy respect for all of the dangers out there.

Those who work toward preparedness will eventually discover it's really just a way of thinking about things. You'll find a true feeling of freedom that comes with putting down a good bet in the favor of the family. If there's nothing else to gain from preparation, the process will instill know-how, a sense of independence and good reason to take some great confidence.

No one counts on disaster, nor would anyone want to rebuild in the aftermath. A common response to life's risks in today's society is to turn your eyes away from a variety of real possibilities. Ignorance is only bliss until reality barges in.

Many people used to save money by putting a little in an envelope whenever possible. Preparation is a similar practice. Preppers can store a few survival materials away and gain some new skills as possible. It builds up quickly.

Readiness offers a better approach to life. You can put aside worries and feel good about your family's position after assembling the proper tools and supplies. There's a certain ease that comes with knowledge, thinking forward and knowing your family is one step ahead of anything Mother Nature could bring. It's simply a matter of planning, thinking and building up a cache of supplies. From there, you could very comfortably hope that you'd never have to collect on your efforts.

Besides holding your pants up, riggers belts are awesome tools that can be used in a multitude of ways.

Every day carry, or EDC, is what we take with us every day, just in case. For some, it is just a cell phone and a credit card. For me, I carry a simple grouping of tools that over the years have evolved into the list on the next page. The evolution started a long time ago with a pocket knife and grew into a refined collection that can help me solve most simple problems that crop up during my typical day.

Depending on what my immediate plans are, I might add to my EDC list with a small hatchet, a bigger knife or a bigger gun. My EDC is enough to stop a fight, not what I would take to war.

This is what the author carries on him every day — a light burden considering the consequences.

- Pen and pad of waterproof paper
- Para-cord survival bracelet
- Belt (nylon web riggers type with steel buckle)
- Cash
- Sunglasses
- Small wind-proof lighter
- Watch
- Handgun

These are the 13 items that on any given day will be on my person. I carry these things because I am comfortable knowing I can mitigate many of the issues I might encounter.

(below) If your eyes or ears require special attention, don't forget that in your preparation plans.

(bottom) Using a pair of good work gloves to protect your hands is a simple and smart decision.

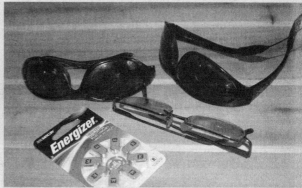

My EDC:

- Larger knife with a lock and at least a 3½-inch blade that can be opened with one hand

- Pocketknife (small slip joint or traditional jack knife)

- Pocket tool carried in a pouch on my belt

- Small single-cell CR123A flashlight

- Small pocket compass

1

STAGES AND LEVELS OF PREPARATION

If you live on the 43rd floor of your building, you should consider that in your emergency plans.

All of us prepare in many ways, for many reasons and for minor and major needs. On the very low end of the scale, preparedness is as inconsequential as looking into your wallet before heading out the door to make sure there's a few dollars inside to pay for lunch. We prepare for the long term with investment plans aimed at creating a decent level of comfort

when retirement age rolls around.

Preparing for the tougher times that any disaster could bring isn't so common to the greater populace, but it still makes a great deal of sense. Tough times happen. There isn't a place on this vast planet that's immune from Mother Nature's worst. Efforts taken now could offer your family a decent degree of comfort even if the greater community struggles amid a catastrophe. It takes some work. It takes some thought. It's time and effort that's very well spent.

Teaching the means and methods of preparation would be a far easier task if it only took a rundown of a few basic strategies, a checklist of required tools and a few brief descriptions on how to use them. Far more people might embark on that important path if a step-by-step blueprint could guarantee they'd survive and thrive in a generic disaster situation. Of course, that's not how the world works.

Preparation requires more than tools and supplies. It requires a proper mindset. It calls for you to pay heed to the smaller intricacies that fall within and contribute to the larger potential problems that any family could face after a disaster. Different problems, meanwhile, require far different solutions.

An earthquake isn't a tornado. A wildfire isn't a flood. And a hurricane isn't a blizzard. No two disasters are identical. Further, different people have different needs.

A few days without electricity would cause anyone some degree of discomfort. It would cause some people far more trouble than others. The elderly man who requires an oxygen machine to live would

A good preparedness plan for a family living in the country will be different than one for a family living in the city.

face a far more critical situation amid even a short-term power outage when compared to the physically fit 32-year-old woman who lives a few houses down the street. We all have different circumstances.

Problems become far more significant for anyone who hasn't prepared as time continues to pass. Supplies dwindle. Patience runs short. Many families, assuredly, would experience a big-time change in attitude and far greater troubles should a few days without electricity stretch into a few weeks.

Building a solid preparation plan that would account for survival and comfort after a disaster is a multi-faceted task. Plans would differ from family to family depending on how the families live. Plans would also look far different based on where various families call home.

Risks, and therefore contingencies, would vary by region. Those in the cold, forested lands of northern Minnesota would obviously leave hurricane shutters out of their preparedness plans. Similarly, those living along the warm beaches of Florida's Gulf Coast aren't going to pack thermal long underwear into their three-day survival kits.

A family's available space and resources would play into their efforts and abilities. A family on a postage-stamp property in the middle of a city will have lesser abilities than others to collect wa-

ter and grow food. They'd certainly have to plan differently than the family living 10 miles out of town on a sprawling, rural plot.

Risks differ in scope and probability depending on where you call home. Some might assess their threats and find comfort in a small-scale preparation plan that would carry a family through a few weeks without having any needs to fulfill from beyond the home. Others might look at the odds and recognize a real potential for significant catastrophe. Those who live in Tornado Alley, for instance, might decide they're more comfortable with plans and supplies that would allow for a few months or more of self-sufficiency.

No guide to preparation could ever claim to provide step-by-step instruction applicable to anyone in any place or for any crisis. Still, all people have the same basic needs. Those who are adept at planning rely on similar thoughts and principles in their efforts to assure wellbeing regardless of their risks.

A good plan will require some tools. Every decent plan will require stocking up in a fashion that most people today haven't considered. Preparedness, however, goes deeper than the contents of the garage, pantry and supply closet. It's a lifestyle.

Those who are best prepared continually work to develop knowledge and new skills that allow them to improvise and make the best use of what's at hand. Means of comfort and survival often come from items bought and stored away. In some cases, those means might come from the environment. The element of unpredictability is bound to become a factor when nature finally decides it's time to put your family to the test. Preparation is always a work in progress.

Your effort might start with settling on your definition of preparation. Frankly, it's a term that isn't given much thought by a good majority of people. For far too many, preparation goes no further than knowing where they'd find the flashlights and a few spare batteries should the lights go down.

There is, of course, the other side. Many people who've heard the term "prepper" probably have some degree of skepticism. They've likely drawn their ideas and a few eyebrow-raising conclusions from news reports or shows on the small handful of folks who live at the far opposite end of the spectrum.

Certainly, there are some people out there with fully loaded shelters carrying several years' worth of food. That group will typically maintain a huge supply of gear and keep their properties well secured. They're often heavily armed. They're often working toward solutions should they find themselves among the lone men and women left walking the planet.

The everyday family would do well for themselves to dismiss the unprepared and hyper-prepared ends of the scale. Most people would assess their level of comfort after thinking about the common, documented risks and find good ways to manage through tough times somewhere in the vast middle ground. Those just beginning preparations should be smart

about planning and keep in mind what you're hoping to accomplish.

When it comes to preparedness, you shouldn't worry about the end of the world. Those preparing for the end of days would eventually have to recognize that any supplies they have in place would eventually run dry. Conversely, it's pretty smart to have the appropriate provisions in place to live comfortably outside your normal, day-to-day lifestyle if hurricanes or tornadoes frequently touch upon your region.

You can get a really good sense of a proper starting point by stopping and looking at your food and water supplies among other provisions. At that point, think about whether you could close the front door, shut down the power and comfortably live for two weeks without leaving the home. When considering all of the potential risks across the country, two weeks provides a pretty reasonable ground floor wherever

Air is the most immediate factor impacting your ability to survive, according to the rule of threes.

you might be. You wouldn't want any less.

Those who are just getting started should let common sense be the guide. Those without any degree of planning are setting up their families to suffer far more than necessary when an emergency comes to bear. Those who planned well in excess of reasonable needs could've probably done better with their time, efforts and money. A level of preparedness that would support safety and comfort after

Shelter requires the greatest immediacy when developing plans to overcome a disaster situation. If your home becomes uninhabitable, you can camp in the yard.

the most typical and even the most serious of documented disasters wouldn't resemble the preparation or lack thereof that sits at either extreme.

I shudder to think about the completely unprepared in light of the documented reality that disaster — whether isolated or wide-scale — affects hundreds of thousands of Americans every year. As for the other side of the scale, I'd suggest preparation shouldn't be all consuming. You shouldn't over-extend your finances for the sake of preparing or let the risks out there affect your ability to enjoy day-to-day life. You shouldn't prepare from a place of fear.

I saw a number of people suffering deeply after Hurricane Katrina who could've had it easier with appropriate forethought and respect for Mother Nature's devastating abilities. As for the opposite end, those who were convinced of approaching cataclysm before the Y2K scare probably ate a lot of rice for an awful long time after that New Year passed quietly. All of us try to live balanced lives. Good preparation fits well within that scope.

Rule of threes

Though potential emergencies vary from place to place, those tackling preparedness have a base-line tool to work from that allows anyone, regardless of circumstances, to consider and build appropriate survival plans. Well-devised plans would also provide some degree of comfort during emergencies, but simply surviving is the foremost goal. You don't need an advanced degree in biology to recognize the human body isn't going to make it too long without food or water.

That's where the rule of threes comes to play. The rule — a list of the elementary factors impacting your ability to survive — sets forth the top priorities and serves as the very foundation of any good planning effort. As grim as it might sound, it's a list that quickly sets forth the very basics of being prepared.

According to the rule, you can live:

- Three minutes without air
- Three hours without shelter
- Three days without water
- Three weeks without food
- Three months without hope

It's the middle three components of the five-fold rule that should command the greatest attention as you begin to assemble your preps. God forbid anyone would be under the water and struggling to find the surface for a three-minute period. In that situation, preparedness efforts wouldn't apply. Further, no tools or strategies would be of assistance should you go without cause for hope over a long period of time.

Shelter carries the greatest immediacy in developing plans to overcome a disaster situation. When considered in terms of the rule, "shelter" doesn't necessarily refer to a structure, or as it's often put, a roof over our heads. It refers to whatever means is used to keep clean and maintain a healthy body temperature. The ability to get a fire started, for instance, would fall under the category of shelter. Some bath-in-a-bag kits would also be considered among shelter planning.

As for water, let's start with a very basic thought: where would the many unprepared among us go to get our daily requirements without all of those faucets that make life so easy? Often enough, emergencies cut off people's ability to draw from their wells or break off their connections to the municipal systems in our urban areas. Water problems might become the very emergency that's left you to rely on your preparations. Situations could rise in which contaminated water is flowing through the pipes that could cause illness if consumed. Water storage and an ability to gather safe water are among the top priorities of a good preparedness plan.

The rule of threes calls for thought about how and what you would eat should a disaster leave the nearby grocery stores boarded up. The rule places lesser priority on food, but remember that it only speaks to how long you could live without. Keeping a pulse and maintaining health and wellbeing are two very different things. Those preparing should consider their own dietary needs while also thinking about how many others they'd need to feed.

The rule of threes, as it speaks to basic survival needs, provides only one half of the vitally important equation. The other side comes in applying your ability to walk that very basic map of survival for various lengths of time should any emergency require it. The rule keeps on moving forward.

If a disaster situation is short term — stretching three days or less — the array of preparations isn't so critical to staying alive but could go a long way toward providing ease until normalcy returns. Those with minimal preparations might find themselves in difficult and stressful, albeit manageable, situations. It might be that a severe thunderstorm downed trees and power lines, leaving a mess of the yard and a widespread set of issues for the power company to manage.

The short-term interruptions that get in the way of everyday living would still require common sense and thought. Those managing through that three-day power outage, for instance, would be wise to stay out of the refrigerator and freezer as much as possible to assure their food supplies don't spoil. The typical, unprepared family would encounter some real stress, but

A few cases of bottled water can go a long way in a disaster situation. It's not too much trouble to keep some on hand at your home.

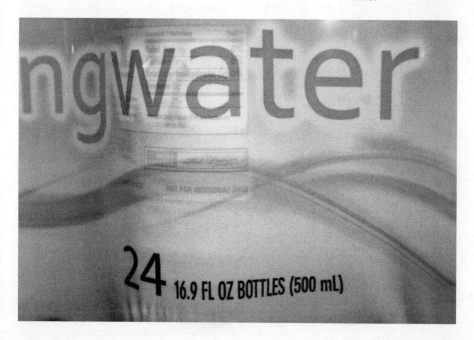

they'd make it through.

Even if a short-term emergency fell right before a normal grocery shopping day, the family is probably going to be alright on food. A home with any degree of insulation would allow a family to meet shelter needs even if by no more ability than blankets and sweatshirts. Those who don't keep additional water for emergencies could have a tougher time, but at that short term, they would still likely have sufficient fluid at hand.

When emergencies stretch longer, it becomes more critical for people to have solid contingencies in place. The level of preparation amid emergency grows more important with every passing day. For every day that a disaster impedes on normal lifestyles, the more people have to rely on themselves and their environments just as people did in earlier eras.

Three days in many ways provides the magic number to consider when assembling your preparations. It's a psychological benchmark. It's at that point when thoughts begin to shift from confidence that a situation will end pretty quickly to a difficult realization that life could be tough for a while. Those worries decrease in equal proportion to your planning. It's also at that point, however, when the rule of threes starts coming into a play at a far more significant level.

Three days is a fairly reliable marker as to when a situation moves from merely inconvenient to presenting genuine difficulties for those who don't have adequate preparations in place. Many would begin to have a rough time at that point even if they still had enough to account for the rule of threes. People are creatures of comfort. Happiness and balance takes more than warmth, food and drink.

Sanitation, for example, could become a critical issue for many unprepared families should a crisis recovery stretch from three days and on toward a few weeks. Morale and confidence could decline for some if the home lost water and the family couldn't flush their toilets by typical means. It's one of many areas of our day-to-day living that doesn't get much thought. People get a better sense of its importance when that luxury isn't there.

After three days, the freezer will start to thaw and put food at risk. Those whose eating habits lean heavily on refrigerated goods could experience some big worry when recognizing all of the grocery stores are closed. Keeping warm would eventually become a true survival issue for the unprepared should an emergency strike in the midst of winter.

It all comes back to the rule of threes. Water requirements provide a good example of the layered challenges that you have to think through in developing a workable plan for a mid-level emergency. Solutions might differ significantly from family to family. The key issue, however, is the same for everyone: those without an ability to secure potable water are at serious risk.

An average person needs to consume about 2 liters of liquid per day to get by. The most short-term of plans just wouldn't suffice as days continue to pass. Those who have only a few jugs of drinking water tucked away for emergency use would watch the supply pass in quick fashion.

Thinking step by step through water's challenges would open up other options beyond having a few 5-gallon jugs stashed away. Concerns decrease as plans grow deeper. I have a hot tub that I could draw water from to flush toilets or wash up. I could run that water through a filter to allow for drinking if it became necessary.

Some would settle on other contingencies. Many don't have hot tubs or swimming pools. Water bladders are available that allow people to store 1,000 gallons or more. Those on large, rural properties might take that option. Of course, it's probably not going to work for those in the cities. Those on smaller lots might purchase a few 55-gallon drums to create some rain barrels.

Walking through that thought process goes to show that regardless of how or where you live, you have the ability to find ways to put your family in a better position to handle a potential disaster. It's simply a matter of untangling all of the many ways a disaster would impede on how we as people typically live and finding ways to account for them. Water is just one piece of the puzzle.

Imagine digging to the very back of the cupboards and realizing there just isn't enough left to prepare a suitable meal. Think about food. Plans for even a period of a couple weeks would require having a suitable supply of shelf-stable goods ready to go.

A move beyond a few weeks of struggles to a matter of months would require even the best prepared to start switching gears. After just so long, you would have to take on an entirely different mindset and focus on sustainable living. Many preppers out there do have food supplies packed away that could last a family for several months. It's not unreasonable. Some go longer. Should a disaster impede community life for months on end, you would eventually have to recognize the new reality and realize your cache isn't going to last forever.

A plan that's stretching beyond the period of several months to a year or more is really no longer about preparation. Should you reach the point of relying on your goods and gear for more than a year, the idea of preparedness would have to give way to a recognition that the community needs to work together for the greater good.

At that point, you truly would have to step back in time and recognize the family's need to hunt, grow food, collect water and account for shelter in the same fashion people did 150 years ago.

It's scary to think about that level of disaster, particularly when compared against the recovery periods after even the most devas-

tating events that have happened of late in the United States. Hurricane Katrina was among the most destructive events of the last century. An evacuated New Orleans was all the same reopened to residents and business owners within weeks of Katrina's landfall. It took far longer to pull that city back to its pre-hurricane condi-

Overcoming disasters like the tornado that hit Joplin, Mo., in 2011 takes extensive planning that accounts for survival and comfort.

tion. In many ways, that process will continue well into the future. All the same, the most critical of infrastructure was restored fairly quickly as evident by the lifted evacuation order.

The period of up to a few months is a reasonable mark to keep in mind when developing your preparations. Disaster inflicts more harm on some than others, but in a community sense, most events only carry disruptions that could impact survival for up to a few weeks. Many preppers wisely assemble the gear and goods necessary to manage through longer periods. More serious events do occur. As is so often said, it's better to be safe than sorry.

Building a solid plan will take time and work. It's also going to cost some money. Anyone who has to stick to a family budget will still have the ability to make preparedness happen.

When applying risks and worst-case scenarios to the rule of threes, preppers will inevitably run across a number of ideas that make a lot of sense for their families. A prepper, for instance, would probably want a large and durable tent should that worst-case event compromise the home or force a quick evacuation. Those aiming for greater comfort in even the most minor of scenarios might want some camping lanterns or Aladdin lamps to provide easy and reliable light sources.

Hand-cranked radios have become a pretty popular option to get that vital information on risks, damages and recovery efforts. The radios might also provide some entertainment when the power goes down. Having a few things at easy reach that can provide some enjoyment and cut the stress shouldn't be overlooked.

In many regards, solid plans come together through a number of smaller costs. A few barrels for water collection would come inexpensively. Assembling a good first aid kit makes all the sense in the world, and it isn't going to break the bank. Those concerned about spending should take the time to honestly assess needs against the rule of threes and then prioritize.

A good preparation plan doesn't happen overnight. Some preppers might find several places where they can make some compromises for the short term. A 5-gallon pail and commode seat, for instance, might suffice in lieu of a $100 camping toilet if the money is needed for a more critical part of the plan.

Some tools would require a fairly sizeable investment. A 5,000-watt generator starts at about $600. It would offer the family the ability to keep the freezer going, use the water-filtration pump and run a

heater. After a good, honest assessment, the cost conscious might determine that a few car batteries and a small inverter would suffice to meet emergency power needs.

My water filtration unit ran about $350. When put against the rule of threes, a reliable filter could become a lifesaver depending on the circumstances brought by an emergency. It was money well spent when placing the cost against the risks.

Many preppers address at least a portion of their food contingencies by purchasing military meals, ready to eat. They're an easy and reliable option given they provide substantial calories and typically have a shelf life of five years or longer. It isn't, however, an inexpensive option to take.

A case of 12 MREs goes for about $70. Those forging plans to sustain for two weeks would probably purchase four cases, or spend $280, per person. It stands to reason that some might look for other less costly, shelf-stable options.

Preparedness is a process that can definitely be as expensive as you want to make it. Costs rise with the length of time that you are looking to provide for self-sufficiency. If you have a goal to go from zero to fully stocked and able for three months of needs, you're going to have to spend an awful lot of money.

You shouldn't feel the need to do so. It might be a matter of getting the biggest bang for the buck by fulfilling a number of smaller, yet important purchases before tackling the big-ticket items. While making the smaller purchases, you might tuck away a few dollars and slowly build it up toward the price of a generator, water filtration unit or the cost of having a wood stove installed in the home.

Simply meeting the ends of survival wouldn't take too much. Minimalist campers provide a great example. They carry very little when heading out on their excursions and often nothing more than what can be kept in a backpack.

The cash-strapped prepper can make big strides by planning wisely. Gardeners could purchase a reliable food dehydrator for the same price as one case of MREs and achieve a good, long-term food solution. They'd be able pack away portions of their annual yields

This is one of the author's bags that is packed with the supplies he needs to survive outside of his home for 72 hours. "Everyone should have at least one," he said.

for fairly substantial periods of time. Those working on tight budgets might consider bartering as an option to get the proper supplies in place. Those of various skills might trade labor so each gets an important task accomplished.

The key point is everyone has the ability to prepare. It's important to remember the first and most vital component to any solid preparedness plan doesn't cost a thin dime. It's learning, thinking and having the ability to break down potential problems.

Step one: a survival mindset

Far and away, the most important tool available during the preparation process and after a disaster isn't available for purchase at the local hardware store. Each of us freely received one. It's the brain. The first goal is to use that amazing tool to its full capability. It starts with recognizing that nothing can be taken for granted. You should come to recognize just how quickly you can run into some pretty serious trouble.

Many have some fairly dramatic ideas on what it would take to put someone in position of fighting for survival. Actually, it doesn't take all that much. It could be as simple as running out of gas in the winter time while driving down a rural road. That driver could very well fall into survival mode if the heater doesn't work and there's a chance another car wouldn't come by for some time.

Preparedness is a matter of recognizing your possible problems and limitations. It's about finding the right answers. It's also a matter of proper attitude. The world's best gear couldn't make up the difference for the person who doesn't have the will or drive to push through the worst that nature or man-made catastrophes could bring. Prepping would make life easier after a disaster, but it won't make life easy.

It reminds me of a fun, family story. Many years back, our family gathered for Thanksgiving dinner. During the course of conversation, someone mentioned the news of a family out West who happened to travel off the main road only to become lost and stranded. As it turned out, the father left the family behind to search for help and ended up dying in the process.

The rest of the family was eventually found, and fortunately, they survived that terrible situation. My youngest son, who was probably about 7 at the time, perked up as we talked and exhibited that confident, survivalist attitude. He said that if that were our family, those who came to the rescue would have found the Nowkas in a warm, comfortable log cabin with plenty of venison to eat.

We laughed. It's still quite funny. The youngster, however, offered up a good example of the determination and confidence you should bring to your planning and to any survival situation. You have to make do with what you have regardless of the situation. From there, it's a matter of drive and working to come out stronger on the other side.

It's far easier on paper or in conversation than it is in reality. Tough situations often require a good deal of willpower. Those with a solid array of preps would still need plenty of mental strength.

I wouldn't think of my time in Haiti after the earthquake as a survival situation. We were given all the supplies we needed. It was nonetheless a difficult situation that demanded a strong and focused mind to meet the challenges brought by that environment. Our meals for that near month consisted solely of MREs. I wouldn't speak poorly of them — they aren't bad by any stretch — but the time eventually

Those without the ability to secure potable water are at serious risk. Rain barrels are an easy way to collect and store water to account for that need.

hits when you would trade just about anything for a good, warm, well-prepared meal.

Looking back, I recognize I would've had an easier time with access to some decent coffee. Sanitation provided some real challenges on the mental level. For that period, all we had were bath-in-a-bag kits as a means of staying clean. There simply wasn't any way to keep clear from the grime given the cloud of dust that permeated everything. We'd wash up before going to bed and would wake up just as filthy as we were before putting our heads on our pillows. It was a pretty taxing experience.

The main point is that gear alone doesn't leave you prepared. It starts and ends with the all-important tool between our ears. Planning requires strategy.

You should recognize the best stockpiles of supplies are meaningless if their goods aren't accessible. Someone stuck out in the woods can't rely on his three-day survival kit if he left it in the closet at home. And those who collected two months of food before the tornado would be in no better shape than their neighbors if the storm picked it up and tossed it 20 miles away.

Preppers need to think about every smaller problem under the umbrella of a disaster. Those who make a home in Tornado Alley might consider some type of under-ground vault that could withstand a tornado. If the worst came to bear, you could pull out your gear and set up camp.

It's easy to fall short in your planning by failing to think through a problem to its very conclusion. While serving in response to Hurricane Ike in Texas, I did a favor to my employer and brought some gear to family members who caught some of the storm but not enough to force evacuation. The

A small survival kit in the glove box of your vehicle might be an afterthought until you really need one. Plan ahead.

home made it through without structural damage, although power lines were down and trees and limbs littered the streets. Given the overall, regional level of destruction, it was going to take some time for life to get back to normal.

On a positive note, that family knew it was important to have a generator as part of their toolkit. The problem, however, came in that they didn't have enough gas on hand to keep it operational, nor enough food or water to make it through the recovery period. It's a good lesson on thinking through from one potential problem to the very next.

As plans develop, so too will confidence. The self-reliant attitude that's fairly unfamiliar to our younger generations still holds pretty strong among many of our older Americans. Not too long ago, an early spring storm that dumped two feet of snow over the course of

an eight-hour period caused plenty of headaches in northern Michigan. The storm knocked down power. It took considerable time for crews to get the streets passable. Temperatures dipped down to the zero mark after the snow stopped falling, and it was a pretty miserable time for a lot of people.

Some homes were left without power for 10 days. A community about 40 minutes south of my home set up a shelter for those affected. Many would expect that much in our modern era. It drew a roll of the eyes from one older gentleman. While talking, he took a tone of surprise and maybe just a bit of contempt at the thought that anyone would rely on a shelter regardless of all the troubles that snowstorm caused. Residents there always got by and never needed that kind of assistance before.

It might just be a matter of where I call home. There were a lot of houses up here that didn't have electricity as recently as 40 years ago. People might be a little bit

These in-ground storage barrels hold important survival materials and will be hidden as part of the landscaping.

tougher in these parts. Certainly, many in the generation before mine were quite self-reliant and didn't have to run into town for every little thing.

The older guy had lived there his whole life. He went through plenty of challenging winters, and it was the first time he could recall anyone needing or seeking that kind of aid. It gives reason for thought. More people would very likely be in far better positions by taking on even a bit of that man's attitude.

The principles of preparation would serve a family well as a community struggles through any disaster's wake. It's not to say your thoughts and efforts have to be tucked away and left until a time of need. An attitude of self-reliance also has its place in the day-to-day.

Self-reliance as it pertains to food means having sustenance at hand that goes beyond what was bagged at the grocery store during the weekend. The food component of a good preparation plan could actually make good economic sense for a family even in typical day-to-day living. You could use some space and a half an hour a day to tend a nice-sized garden.

Growing food is inexpensive and lends to a healthy way of living. I enjoy fresh vegetables year-round. I'm not as fond of having them shipped in from around the world when the growing season is over.

I'm OK with packing some green beans in the freezer and doing some canning. Gardening requires some room, but many even with smaller properties could make it happen. You might not grow a full year's worth of vegetables, but even a few months of food is worth the effort.

Some of those living in the city might determine the well-manicured backyard offers nothing more than a weekly mowing chore. That space might get better use as a garden. Those living in rural areas would find there's little less expensive than raising chickens. They provide perfect protein in the form of their eggs every day of the week.

Self-reliance extends beyond food. It comes down to the little things. Those dedicated to preparedness often find it really isn't something separate from the rest of their lives. It just becomes part of their way of living.

For instance, I have a small compass on my key ring and keep a pocketknife and small flashlight with me. It's just part of what I do. I'm more comfortable that way. Some preppers put down significant sums on gear only to pack it away. Those who use pieces of their preparation on a regular basis are making a far better investment.

My water filtration unit, for instance, is in my kitchen. It gets daily use. My coffer maker requires filtered water. My wife uses it for drinking water.

I mentioned Aladdin lamps as a good source of light in a short-term emergency situation. The lamps have another role in my home. I simply enjoy them. I've always had interest in functional art, and I have about a dozen Aladdin oil lamps in different rooms in my home.

Certainly, they're preps, but their history is fascinating, and many of the lamps are quite beautiful works. Many feature glass, nickel and brass. Several have ornate features.

The lamps are tremendous tools from a prepper's standpoint as they offer light and also create warmth. They're tools that give a boost to my attitude. Few take any degree of pleasure when the power goes down. When the time comes to use my lamps, I'm excited about the opportunity.

There are plenty of opportunities to take what you're already doing and make it part of your preparedness. Those who barbecue as a hobby could do a bit of reading and experimentation and quickly learn how to smoke fish. It would open a great source of preserved protein should a disaster impact food supplies.

Hunters aren't heading into the field hoping to add to their longer-term plans, but in one sense, they're doing precisely that. Those who enjoy gardening are exercising self-reliance, but might not see it that way. It's just part of their lifestyles. The hobbyist with basic car repair abilities has a solid self-reliance skill that could come in handy quickly during an emergency.

Preparation at the onset requires thoughts and efforts that many haven't considered before. It becomes more natural. As the process moves forward, preppers will come to find it's just become a part of who they are. Preppers become more self-reliant as preparations begin to unfold and it begins to show in their day-to-day lives.

Living in preparedness offers some peace of mind when understanding the risks around us. It makes a lot of sense to extend your self-reliant attitude beyond concerns for what could happen. Those who live with their preparations might have lesser stress when troubles actually strike. They're already in the mode to handle it in a calm and well-thought-out manner.

Preparing takes gear and supplies, but it's far more a practice in mindset. As you develop a self-reliant attitude, the ideas of "survival" and "preparation" become smaller. An understanding of preparation as "just our way of life" grows in equal proportion.

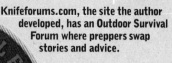

No one expert could ever claim to have all the answers when it comes to good preparedness. All plans share some basics, though no two well-developed plans could ever look the same. Every person is different. Every family is unique.

Many plans can nonetheless improve by sharing ideas.

Fortunately, there is a wealth of resources out there offering a variety of potential solutions for you to draw from when building the right plan for your family. Websites, magazines and even television could provide you with thoughts on potential problems and a number of good solutions that hadn't previously come to mind.

Living Ready Magazine, a magazine that is published quarterly by F+W Media, is another great resource for preppers.

Those just getting started might scroll through the information available at www.ready.gov. It's a website maintained by the Federal Emergency Management Agency, and it provides good information on an extensive list of topics related to disasters, preparedness, health and safety. It's a great start. You could do better than the bare minimum prepping recommendations typically offered on the site though.

Any number of online forums are out there and accessible through simple searches, whether for "survival," "prepping" or "preparation." Some information might be useful to the individual prepper. Some would prove useless. It would

differ by the family and its plan. They're good places to check out to see what other preppers are doing. Occasionally, you will stumble across ideas that apply well to your own effort.

Knifeforums.com, the site I developed, has a solid section dedicated to preparedness. *Living Ready*, a magazine published quarterly by F+W Media, is another great resource that provides a variety of tips and thoughts for the average folks who value preparedness but aren't so much worried about the end of days.

You might not live on the fringe or have any intention of heading there. It still doesn't hurt to take a look at all the solutions those hyper-dedicated preppers devised. Doomsday Preppers, which airs on the National Geographic Channel, might be off-putting to some and might unfortunately play into a stigma toward the idea of readiness. You shouldn't throw out the baby with the bathwater though. You might not ascribe to the views or fears of those documented, but you might still catch onto an idea or two that solves an issue in your own planning from those efforts.

The very point is to gather from the big pool of knowledge out there and consider the bits that fit best into your preparedness efforts. It doesn't matter where they come from. No one but each individual prepper could possibly know what'll work best for his family. Prepping is a multi-faceted effort that takes a lot of learning in a number of different areas. Based on its vast scope, it's extremely valuable to get a sense of how others are accounting for their variety of needs.

2

STAYING PUT

Your home is the very definition of comfort.
In a disaster situation, it's often best to
stay where you are.

As it's often been said, "there's no place like home." It's a cliché that certainly rings true for those dealing with the aftermath of a disaster. Home provides the very definition of comfort.

Home certainly stands to become a less peaceful place when a family is left without power. There might be structural damage. A home isn't

so cozy when a portion of the roof caves to the weight of a toppled tree. The yard might become a nest of tangled branches and downed utility lines.

The work ahead might be daunting, but it's still the family's most familiar place. It's a common point that bonds the family. It provides an advantage that can't be overstated amid the inevitable stress brought on by catastrophe.

Home is a great headquarters for recovery in a very practical sense. The home is where the gear is kept. An organized prepper could grab a flashlight, head into the darkened workshop and find the precise tool needed for any job. Much of your plans should be built with the home in mind.

Families that made appropriate preparation efforts will have meals tucked away in their food lockers that'll keep everyone well fed for a good amount of time. Those who've assembled the right tools and supplies should have an ability to stay warm and dry and have plenty to drink as the community at large slowly heals from its bruises.

Your home is a great headquarters for recovery in a disaster situation. Your emergency plans should be built with the home in mind.

Our homes are indeed our castles. You might question why a family would ever evacuate. The answer is clear and simple. A prepper shouldn't focus his top concerns on the days or weeks after nature shows its power. He should worry most about the very disaster itself.

Safety is the first goal, and it therefore makes the most sense to get away from impending danger if it's reasonably possible. Preppers should pay close attention to any forewarning of approaching dangers and make quick, reasoned decisions. Sometimes, it's safer to bug out. Often, warnings are insufficient and leave you no choice but to stay in place and make use of all the tools and supplies you've stashed away.

The key is to make a smart and unemotional decision. It's easy to imagine a prepper getting stubborn and taking on a hold-his-ground kind of attitude, particularly with all the time and money spent to account for food, water and gear. Someone who spent a good chunk of a paycheck on a generator and built up a good supply of gas might figure it's finally time to put it to use. A person of this mindset is missing the point of preparedness. A plan isn't about stuff. Instead, it's all that stuff that supports the plan.

The greater point of prepared-ness is exercising the forethought necessary to make it through whatever the world puts in your way and by the best possible means. Home is comfort. Safety, however, should always trump ease and abundance. Imagine all of the second guessing that would come should a family member suffer a significant injury due to a weather event. To put it even more bluntly, there wouldn't be anything more uncomfortable than having to mourn a lost life.

The home is sometimes the safest place to be. Quite often, there's no reasonable way to steer away from danger. The decision to huddle into the basement safe room is often made by Mother Nature when events such as tornadoes or even severe thunderstorms carrying tremen-dous straight-line winds bear down quickly.

There's no good way to out-run the severe winter weather many across the northern sections of our country are familiar with. Remaining at home is often the best decision.

A family would need appropriate food and water to stay in their home following a disaster. This food storage room was designed by the American Preparedness Center, LLC.

This food storage room designed by American Preparedness Center, LLC was an unusable crawl space before the project.

Mother Nature can get ugly pretty quickly. People have an average of only 14 minutes to find a place of safety when tornadoes threaten, according to the National Oceanic and Atmospheric Administration. There isn't time for anything but accounting for the family members and pets and scrambling to the very nearest place of safety. Those experiencing tornadoes could draw envy from some for having even that short bit of notice. Those living near fault lines are typically caught by complete surprise when the planet's inner workings decide it's time for an earthquake to unleash its destruction.

Preparing for a stay-in-place recovery requires a cache of supplies that'll firmly account for the rule of threes. A family would need appropriate food and water. Shelter considerations would vary significantly

Shelter considerations vary significantly depending on the region you live in and its risk factors.

Cooking without electricity might require a simple camp stove. The author bought these three from yard sales for $5 or less each.

sions to keep the kids' minds occupied should they lose their computers, TVs and video game systems.

depending on the region and its risk factors. Some would account for cold. Some would account for ways to manage through extreme heat. Some thoughts are fairly general and would apply to everyone. Others are pinpointed based on what history can tell a prepper. The planning process for those at reasonable risk of tornadoes, for instance, should include some considerable thought on how their families would manage through a complete loss of home.

A good plan would include a variety of items that extend beyond the rule of threes. Survival is the top goal, but comfort can be accomplished after that basic foundation of preparedness is laid. Additional efforts would focus on how to keep life as normal as possible during any periods of upheaval.

Comfort would mean lighting. It might include a method of cooking. Those with kids at home would be wise to have any number of diver-

Planning isn't a process aimed at making a recovery easy. No degree of preparation could offer that kind of guarantee. Those who plan thoughtfully and completely, however, are taking steps that would make the aftermath of a disaster far more manageable. A well-prepared family would be better equipped to take their troubles in stride.

Destructive events would be tough in some degree on anyone. Even those managing recovery from the comfort of home would watch their patience wilt away. A prepper might find a silver lining in knowing that recovery mechanisms in place today are far greater than those that were available to struggling communities in decades past.

The world has become smaller, and thus, help is never far from materializing. Those charged with recovery aid have never been better planned. Modern technology with all of its more troublesome impacts has also made life safer and recovery efforts far more efficient.

Emergency relief in today's world starts within minutes. The first outside aid often arrives within hours. Supplies and manpower regularly build to significant levels in a matter of days. Government agencies, humanitarian organizations and even those in the private sector can mobilize quickly. Relief agencies, with the benefit of advanced warning, will often have aid ready and available before troubles strike. The American Red Cross, for instance, had nearly 2,400 volunteer workers in the Gulf Coast in 2012 before Hurricane Isaac made its late-August landfall. They had almost 290,000 meals ready to go as communities still waited on the storm's arrival.

Improvements to emergency response means the days of long-term, concerted efforts to stay on the right side of the rule of threes after a destructive event aren't as likely as they used to be. Relief workers make health and safety their top priorities. Given the strength of our communication systems, it would take an unbelievably large and wide-scale event for any community of people to go unnoticed or left to fend for itself for any significant length of time.

Of course, there's no such thing as the perfect response. Recover-ies still lag from time to time. Yet, outside of the most catastrophic disasters, the detailed level of coordination and planning in place throughout the country often leads to timely restoration of a community's critical infrastructure.

Abilities vary depending on the unique aspects of any disaster. Crews, however, can often make reasonably quick work of delivering a safe water supply, restoring electric power distribution and assuring adequate medical resources. As each piece of that infrastructure comes back on line, those affected can rely that much less on the tools and supplies assembled as part of their own preparation plans.

The nation's power companies provide vivid illustration of the quick efforts that lend toward relief. Several, wide-scale destructive events testify to the industry's preparedness and the skill of its workers in identifying and solving problems. A glance at power outage statistics when comparing the depth of destruction to the eventual restoration times is often pretty amazing.

More than 18,000 customers were left without power after the deadly and destructive 2011 tornado that tore through Joplin, Mo. Within a week, 10,000 of those customers had their power back, according to U.S. Department of Energy reports. In 2012, Hurricane

Isaac knocked out power to nearly 900,000 homes in Louisiana after its landfall. All but 6,200 customers had their power restored within nine days. In 2004, more than 2 million Florida customers were left without electricity after Hurricane Charley made landfall. Within 10 days, 95 percent of those customers had their power restored.

Improvements have been notable in a number of categories. The United States, from local government units to the federal level, has come a long way in just a matter of a few years. It's another silver lining, and it truly cast its glow off the darkest of clouds. The American public in many ways came to its far stronger position by virtue of some tremendous hardship that added sorrow to the most recent chapters of our history. In the wake of tragedy, the government — along with private entities — worked hard to quickly and vastly improve capabilities to benefit post-disaster recovery efforts.

The attacks of Sept. 11, 2001 changed so much about our country. It wasn't only an attack on New York, Washington and those who lost their lives in Pennsylvania. It was an attack on each and every American. Though we'd all like to go back and change that terrible day, the truth of the matter is we're

Building a small underground storage/storm shelter is a reasonable way to keep your survival or recovery supplies safe as long as you are in an area that does not flood.

far safer now because of it.

The best and brightest got to work in the wake of that unprecedented assault on our nation and its way of life. Detailed contingency planning came together from the smallest of localities all the way through major, federal-level agencies. Those with roles in emergency response became more focused and placed greater emphasis on meeting across disciplines and jurisdictional lines. They walked through risks, discussed vulnerabilities and figured out solutions. Though efforts were designed around terrorism risks and responses, many aspects of that planning apply just as well to disaster recovery in all forms.

Improvements touched every corner of the country. Police and fire departments serving the gamut from rural townships to the largest cities obtained new tools and training that weren't always feasible for communities amid continually tight, local budgets. The emergency crews that had long recognized their own weaknesses had the ability to apply for grants, and very few of those requests were turned down. The attacks ushered in a completely new era of vigilance.

Despite all of those efforts, the mess and turmoil left in the wake of Hurricane Katrina almost four years later managed to highlight a new series of weaknesses. Ire and disbelief built quickly across the country through detailed media reports of what can still be regarded as a debacle. It left officials no choice but to make quick and significant improvements. Many couldn't believe such a situation could happen here in America.

Improper long-term planning combined with poor decisions and a lack of coordination at all levels only exacerbated the difficulties created by that intense and powerful storm. In the wake of the disaster, Congress passed several laws aimed at improving disaster response. The Federal Emergency Management Agency underwent a number of changes based on its poor performance in the aftermath. Humanitarian organizations reflected on their responses, re-assessed capabilities and made their own changes, including heightened volunteer training and increased collaboration.

Today, relief workers' abilities to hasten healing are stronger than ever, and they continue to grow. Hurricane Katrina and the attacks of Sept. 11, 2001 remain fresh on the minds of many. The devastation brought by Superstorm Sandy in 2012 only strengthened resolve as vulnerabilities showed face once again. The country hasn't let down its guard.

Any level of emergency response improvement shouldn't be enough for any family to let down its own guard. Preparing is a recognition that the individual can do better than hope for the best and wait on whatever aid might come from others. Recent improvements don't diminish the need for vigilance in each and every household. Truthfully, our overall capabilities as a nation would improve to a yet greater level if more people exercised forethought and properly

If you have the ability to generate your own power during a blackout, even if it is just a little bit, staying at home becomes much easier.

accounted for their own family's needs.

Efficient and improving response from outside sources doesn't mean instantaneous relief after the weather calms. There will always be some degree of chaos and a lot of struggling early after any disaster as workers assemble, sort through the mess, determine needs and finally begin to get a handle on the disarray. A more efficient system is little consolation to those facing the greatest, immediate struggles.

Growing capabilities after disasters have not and could not overcome the benefits of proper planning. Care provided for the masses could never account for the unique considerations of any individual. Your property, with the benefit of a preparedness plan, would inevitably provide greater amenity and an all-important level of privacy you wouldn't find at the large-scale community shelter.

Having a kitchen, living room and just a few small bedrooms wouldn't seem like much for the young family in a starter home getting by in typical calm. You would gain a far greater appreciation though if you're forced to take up a small place among hundreds of cots unfolded in a high school gym. Prepping goes beyond environment. Having food at easy reach is better for your spirit, confidence and sense of normalcy than having

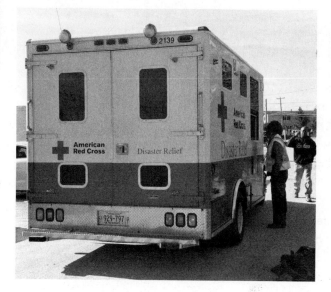

just getting started with a preparation plan is, "How much is enough?" Unfortunately, it's a question that's difficult to answer. It would be different for many people. Relief workers, as any number of disasters have shown, focus their earliest efforts on the infrastructure that would vitally impact the rule of threes. Major needs reaching the greater numbers in a community are often met with haste.

Relief, however, doesn't always come at once. A family whose home was damaged and pushed off its foundation would need a greater plan than the nearby family that only has debris to clear. Crews might restore electricity to 90 percent of an affected community within three days, but it could take three additional days to get through that next 5 percent. It could be a week beyond that or longer to address the last few darkened homes and businesses with unique issues.

Dedicated preppers will extend their preparedness plans beyond

to stand in line for whatever meals are being served by relief workers that day.

Those who undertake preparation do so in recognizing that while many hope for the best, there's greater strength in taking the right actions to make the best happen. Preparing eliminates the need to rely, hope or wait. What's needed is there and ready.

Preparedness is an exercise aimed at getting through any rough period with as little difficulty as possible. Our relief organizations are generous, well intentioned, caring and do tremendous work to lift up those at their points of greatest need. None of them, however, could understand your families' needs and worries as well as you do. That's where prepping comes into play.

A common question among those

the timeframe of a few weeks in recognizing that there are always exceptions to the typical. Preparing at its most basic is a matter of being ready for the exceptional. We set two weeks at a minimum baseline in recognition that disasters happen often enough that they could impact typical services at some level for that length of time.

Deeper plans provide greater insurance. If the full extent of those efforts is never needed, it would still stand to provide the prepper with greater peace of mind. A family that's regrouping in the early hours after disaster could never know with certainty whether businesses and services

Make your plan part of your everyday life. This Aladdin lamp is functional without electricity and is also art.

would be up and running after three days. Adequate repairs and untangling the complex problems ushered in by disaster could just as well take three weeks.

The mess beyond the door might appear unworkable. Some could certainly take joy if normalcy started returning quickly. Should the exceptional come to pass, those who built their plans even a little bit deeper could at least feel some relief knowing needs would be covered.

The home itself is indeed a valuable tool in an overall preparation scheme should circumstance mean you must stay in place. Familiarity provides more to those recovering from emergencies than some might think. You would be hard pressed to think of another locale in which you could walk from an upstairs bedroom to the first-floor kitchen in the dark without having to feel around or risk stubbing a toe on the furniture.

Residents know where to find their valves, sockets and breaker switches. There are valuable safety and convenience factors at play. It's also a matter of efficiency. Staying in place affords you the ability to recover more quickly after trouble passes. Those affected by destructive forces can't clear away the damages if they're on the road or camping out 100 miles away.

The home, conversely, can

become a dangerous temptation for many. Both preppers and non-preppers are often too rigid to give safety its due position over everyday comfort. Recent events have shown the dangers that can come from an ill-placed decision to stay in place, whether it comes from a place of gambling, stubbornness or naiveté.

Hurricanes Katrina and Isaac and Superstorm Sandy each provided examples. Sizable populations settled in during each despite clear, forewarned dangers. It's beyond common sense. Those who nonetheless carry a strong determination to stay in place regardless of any approaching danger should at least try to account for safety by some method and well in advance. A prepper in the southernmost stretches of Mississippi or Louisiana who's dead set and would refuse to pack up and move on might at least install an escape hatch in the attic. It would only make sense after watching the many rooftop rescues amid dangerously high floodwaters.

The majority of your preps would come to play after the danger has passed and it's time to get a handle on any damage. A prepper's life would probably be all right after the event passes as long as everyone made it through safely. Life might not be simple after that point, but it's still living. After calm returns, it's a matter of getting by as best as you are able until the rest of the community catches back up.

Families might not rely on outside help but would all the same hold confidence in their professionalism. Recent history has shown how planning and collaboration contribute to the needs of those suffering. Response to the Joplin tornado included a host of agencies — both local and from beyond — that provided urgent aid to the tattered community.

The storm left incredible destruction and heartache behind it. The mile-wide tornado tore across 22 miles of terrain and brought winds topping 200 mph. A 6-mile stretch of that path went right through the center of the city.

The tornado destroyed nearly 7,000 houses as well as schools, churches, stores and other buildings. Structures have been replaced. The greater tragedy was the 161 people who were killed in the tornado. The storm injured nearly 1,400 more. It was the deadliest tornado since 1947 and the seventh deadliest in U.S. history.

Efforts were nearly instantaneous. It started local and grew. Ambulances were at work within 10 minutes, and a small army of EMS workers was moving through the community within a half hour. Missouri's governor brought in members of the National Guard the very same day to aid efforts in Joplin as well as other areas of the state impacted that day by storms. By the next day, a Missouri FEMA task force was on hand in Joplin to provide search and rescue expertise.

More people might take the examples of vigilance shown at government and organizational levels and scale it down to their own homes. Tornadoes are among the clearest, most frequent examples of emergencies in which you would want to move away but reasonably couldn't do so. Authorities have recommended sheltering in place for short-term chemical disasters and, most notably, those that offer no time for safe evacuation. Families might buckle down inside their homes, rely on their preparations and treat their properties as islands should pandemic illnesses strike.

Severe snowstorms are a good example of the potential emergency in which most people would make the reasoned decision to settle in at home until it blows over. The worst of storms might require patience and create some share of difficulty. Power outages are common and sometimes stretch for days. Transportation often grinds to a halt. Those storms could very literally create roadblocks for police, firefighters and other emergency crews.

Snowstorms, though, are rarely destructive on a large scale. Further, there's no good way to outrun severe winter weather. Storms can shift quickly. Sometimes, they're large and widespread enough to impact any number of states, much less a few communities or counties. There's really no good reason a well-prepared family would consider leaving in that type of scenario.

Some components of preparedness do take account for the very moments of danger. The inescapable risks in any region should give families particular cause

There are hundreds of books and other resources that are helpful and interesting for those making emergency plans.

to think through any means available to prevent harm. Safety comes first.

The risk of tornadoes is a significant one for large portions of the country. People in regions that see them frequently should, at a minimum, make sure each member of the family is well versed in safety recommendations whether at home, on the road or otherwise away from any suitable structure. As risks grow, so too should contingencies.

Proper forethought and protective actions can make up for some of what's lost by a lack of time when dangers roll in and strike quickly. Anyone living in Tornado Alley would be wise to construct a safe room in their homes to provide protection. It's recommended that people build their safe rooms in their basements. Those without basements could reinforce an interior room on the first floor to serve that purpose.

Simply defined, a safe room is windowless room built of concrete walls and a concrete ceiling that can withstand the high winds of even the strongest tornadoes. It's a prep that comes with significant cost. If a family is at a significant enough risk, you really couldn't put a price tag on your life or those of your loved ones.

Those at greatest risk of tornadoes should consider stocking

those safe rooms with three or four months' worth of food for each member of the family to account for the

It's important to have some fun once you get settled in after a disaster strikes.

worst case. Having adequate supplies would also mean a couple durable tents. If the home around the safe room toppled in a tornado, the family could leave that room, dust off and quickly set up camp. From there, the family could get right to the task of clean-up efforts.

Those without the financial means to build a safe room should at least identify the areas of their homes where they'd be safest in the event of a tornado, whether it's the basement, bathtub or a first-level coat closet. You should at the very least consider a way to keep the family's preparation gear in a place that's accessible and wouldn't be blown two counties away. A small, waterproof, underground storage spot would serve that purpose. You could meet that goal by different methods and often at minimal expense.

Vigilance is truly the most important tool in the kit and could very well become the difference that separates life and death. A family should consider having a weather alert radio in the home. It isn't a tool by which you could place full confidence. Forecasting isn't a precise, foolproof science. Still, it's a means of receiving information on watches and warnings at the very moment they're issued.

Meteorologists can provide significant advanced notice when conditions open up the possibility for tornadoes. They're able to provide general, regional outlooks on tornado risks for a week or more ahead. A prepper in an area at risk for tornadoes would be well served by paying attention to those outlooks and responding appropriately.

If the weather forecast indicates severe weather and potential tornado risk, you could enhance the safety of your home and others in the neighborhood by heading out and getting the yard cleaned up. A vigilant prepper would take notice and get all of the kids' toys out of the backyard and the garden tools put away. You don't need a full-scale, definite tornado warning to think about the items a cyclone would turn into projectiles.

It's vital to act quickly on the best information available. Surveys conducted by NOAA in the aftermath of the 2011 Joplin disaster determined that a majority of people failed to respond in prompt fashion. Many failed to take appropriate shelter when the initial warning was issued. Through surveys, officials learned some complacency set in given the frequency that sirens sound in that region. In Tornado Alley, it makes sense that sirens would sound often. Too many people didn't worry about the siren's blare based on past experiences in which little danger materialized after the warnings.

There's no way to determine how many lives could've been saved or injuries spared had more people in Joplin acted with appropriate haste. Some quickly took the best shelter available and still sustained injuries or lost their lives. It was a monstrous, once-in-a-generation kind of storm. Preppers wouldn't take chances. It's tough to think about the prospect of a critical, potentially fatal situation and realize more could've been done for the sake of safety. Nature deserves our respect.

Every minute matters and each provides better odds to any family. Even the limited time offered by warnings today is so much more than our forefathers had. Whether it's sonar or radar technology or satellite imagery, there's often sufficient warning of threatening events so that people can at least take cover if it's not possible to get away. Those who lived generations ago had no more warning than their own eyes and best senses as dark clouds and pressure changes came over. Though advance notice of tornadoes only averages 14 minutes, it's a major step forward. The average advance warning for tornadoes was only about five minutes in the early 1990s, NOAA reports.

The warning system isn't perfect. Meteorologists are sometimes caught by surprise just like the rest of us. Occasionally, there are still reports of tornadoes touching ground without any prior emergency warning.

The advanced system is frequently a lifesaver. It isn't likely we'll see as many mass casualty tornadoes as we did generations ago. Warnings have improved and so many people are plugged in. Consider it one more solid point in technology's positive column. Whether it's the cell phones or the televisions stationed everywhere, you are likely to learn about watches and warnings wherever you might be.

In spite of the best technologies, some events, by virtue of their size, lack of sufficient warning or both, will still cause some deaths along their paths of destruction. History, however, speaks well of the nation's growing readiness. Among the top 10 deadliest documented tornadoes in the United States, Joplin's storm was the lone to occur after 1953.

Earthquakes provide another key example of why forethought and safety planning are among the most important aspects of your preparedness. For all the advances in recent years, scientists still haven't figured out a method to accurately pinpoint when and where an **If you decide to stay, make sure you are ready. Otherwise long lines could be in your future.**

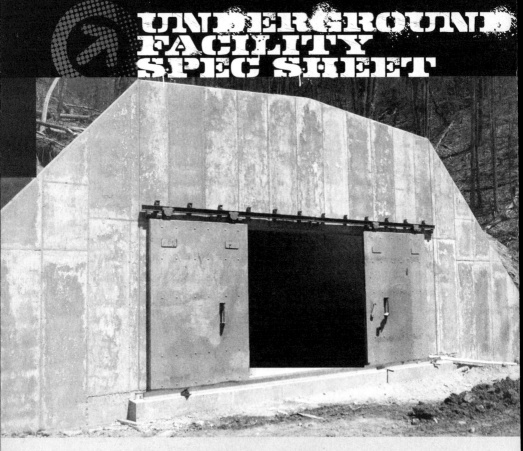

The American Preparedness Center Built this shelter for a private individual. If you have your own mountain (purchased separately), you can build one of these for the low price of $750,000.

- 1,900 square feet

- 1,080 square feet living area

- Remaining space is garage, walkway and generator room

- Designed to support 8 people

- 18-inch re-enforced concrete side walls with No. 6 and No. 9 size re-bar every 10 inches

- 30-inch re-enforced concrete floor with No. 6 and No. 9 size re-bar every 10 inches

- 30-inch re-enforced concrete roof

with No. 6 and No. 9 size re-bar every 10 inches

- 7,000-psi-rated concrete

- Every batch/load of concrete was tested by an inspector to confirm all loads met spec

- Exposed and covered concrete is covered with ¼-inch thick waterproof rubber coating

- Total of 483 yards of concrete

- 2¼-inch steel-wrapped, sliding, concrete-filled blast doors for garage

- 3¼-inch steel-wrapped, concrete-filled blast doors (inside)

- 1 back pressure blow out valve (inside garage to main facility-located above internal blast door)

- 2 sleeping rooms

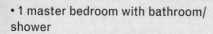

- 1 master bedroom with bathroom/shower
- 1 main bathroom/shower
- 1 ventilation room
- 1 power and storage room
- 1 main common area
- 1 1,000-gallon diesel tank
- 1 1,000-gallon water tank
- 1 built-in water filtration system
- Built into a mountainside. Will cover entire structure except for garage entrance with roughly 20 inches of dirt.
- Escape hatch in master bedroom
- Built for up to 8 people
- LED lighting

earthquake will strike or at what magnitude. There certainly isn't any way to declare approaching peril in a manner that could get a population out of the way before the earth begins rumbling. The unpredictability of earthquakes goes to explain the severe tolls they've taken even in very recent times.

The 2010 earthquake in Haiti took the lives of 316,000 people. The quake injured another 300,000 people and left about 1 million homeless. Having worked in its aftermath, I can't imagine seeing a greater level of destruction. From 2000 to 2010, there were four quakes around the world that took the lives of 50,000 or more people, according to the United States Geological Survey. Just two years before the Haiti disaster, an earthquake in the Sichuan region of China killed more than 87,000 people and injured 374,000.

The lack of advance warning as it pertains to earthquakes isn't a matter of socioeconomics or money spent on science and forecasting in any given country. The United States, with all of its research funding, is as vulnerable to the abrupt nature of dangerous tremors as anywhere else. Think back to the 1989 Loma Prieta earthquake that killed 63 people and injured more than 3,700 others in northern California. Its initial jolt came while thousands of fans were already in their seats at San Francisco's Candlestick Park in anticipation of a World Series game that was to begin a half hour later.

The stadium made it through the jolt. Baseball fans made it to safety. They played the game 10 days later. Only by a stroke of fortune, a terrible catastrophe didn't become worse.

Those in regions where earthquakes are more typical should also be able to identify the safest places in their homes. Current FEMA recommendations suggest climbing beneath a sturdy table. If that isn't available, FEMA recommendations advise crouching and covering your head in an inside corner of the structure. Those outdoors should get away from buildings, wires and streetlights.

Those at any reasonable risk of earthquake shouldn't keep anything heavy tucked up on high shelves. Glass items should be kept in latched cabinets and shelving should be secured to walls. Should tremors come out of nowhere, those bits of forethought would lessen the potential for injuries.

Stay-at-home planning regardless of the potential danger at question will require some education. Knowing the unfathomable work heaped on emergency responders in the earliest hours after a disaster, every prepper should know the basics of first aid. The efforts necessary to build up to meet a community's needs take less time than ever before, but it still takes crucial time.

Your family's aftermath might be far different than that of another down the street or the neighbors around the corner. Some might emerge from the basement or crawl space after a storm to find the home crumbling around them. Others might come out to find little, if any damage. The severity of damage left by any disaster could differ tremendously from one city block to the next.

It's a lottery for many. It isn't for the prepper. It would become a matter of using the gear and goods at ready to account for the new, albeit temporary, reality.

Anyone should consider a strong tent or two at the ready for use as a temporary home. It's fair to hope your hardest that the tents are only ever used for camping excursions. You should plan additional, related provisions that could appropriately make those tents feel somewhat like home. You would want some decent sleeping bags and lanterns,

but you also might consider items like air mattresses among other goods.

Pack food. Store some water. Have the ability to collect water and make water potable.

The rule of threes is the start. Getting the home ready through preparation beyond the very basics takes a variety of thoughts and decisions. There are different methods available to achieve a prepper's many goals. Solutions would differ from prepper to prepper.

If you have a generator as part of your plan, make sure you have enough gas on hand to make it useful should an emergency event stretch on for a number of days. It's difficult to predict what amounts would suffice. You wouldn't want more than you can continually cycle through whether via the lawnmow-

Having some extra gas on hand could save you a lot of time and money in a disaster situation. Plan ahead for what your generator will need.

Buying a generator could be a daunting task for those who aren't sure about what they'll need. From low-end to high-end, there are plenty of options. Those looking to buy on the cheap could find any number of low-wattage units in the $300 range. Then again, you shouldn't spend money on an item that would fail to meet your needs. Those who have several thousands of dollars to spend would find generator systems on the market that would bring the home — regardless of size — back to full power at the first flicker of a power outage. Those purchasing for emergency purposes wouldn't have to go that far.

I'd suggest a 5,000-watt generator. They typically fall in the $500 to $700 range. It'll provide enough power to run the water pump, keep the refrigerator running and put a chill on the freezer when needed. It would still have enough capacity to power up a few lights. It's enough to meet basic needs during a short- to mid-term stretch without electricity.

The 5,000-watt unit might not account for wants, but if the power is down, those bits of comfort might not be available, anyhow. Those thinking about a unit that would also power up a television might consider the fact that access to cable or satellite systems would also likely be compromised. Those concerned about having enough light could light up a few Coleman lanterns or Aladdin lamps to complement what they're able to achieve from the generator.

It's wise to test your generator once a month by starting it up and letting it run for an hour with a couple light bulbs turned on.

Keep the generator outside to avoid the risk of carbon monoxide poisoning. An owner should spend due time with the manual to assure comfort and proper usage.

Don't overload it. You should pay close attention to what you're powering. Remember Ohm's law as a means to assure items in use remain within the generator's capacity. Volts multiplied by amps provides wattage.

Think about safety. Those planning to hook up their generators for access to outlets should make sure to completely disconnect the home from the power grid. Those who fail to do so would send electricity back through the line, which would present dangers to those out working.

Using the outlets isn't necessary. Get a model that includes wheels and purchase some lengthy, heavy duty extension cords. It might not be as convenient, but it's a good solution if you are only focusing on needs.

As for maintenance, it's smart to start up the generator once a month and let it run for an hour with a couple light bulbs turned on. A prepper wouldn't want to have an engine that doesn't start when a moment of need finally arrives. It only takes a moment to pull the cord. As for preparedness, those with generators should make sure to have enough gas on hand to meet their preparedness goals. I keep about 15 gallons handy, but remember to use it and replenish. Gas isn't good forever.

er, snow blower or otherwise. You might consider emptying gas cans into the car after a certain amount of time. Gas goes bad after a while. You should recognize that factor and figure out how to account for it as part of your planning.

Some families, whether out of interests in preparation, environmentalism or both, would forego the gas-powered generator and rely on a different way to secure electricity. Some might install solar panels or build wind generators. They're pricy in terms of initial investment, but they offer an ability to recoup. Often, such systems will allow people to take the furnace, water heater or other expensive necessities off the grid, and by proxy, off the electric bill. They'd also have the ability to keep in stride while neighbors do without after emergency.

Families should prepare in some manner for the possibility of criminal activity in the aftermath of any disastrous event. It isn't the greatest of concerns, but it's still worth some degree of thought. In that sense and in many others, an element of preparedness is keeping a good relationship with neighbors. Everyone needs allies. It makes the best sense to have those at your closest proximity on your side.

Often, the best protection you can have for your home is the watchful eyes of the people who live around you. There's a good reason why police departments so heavily encourage the organization of neighborhood watch groups. Criminals rely on opportunity, and the smart ones know better than to head into those active neighborhoods that have any number of eyes looking out for suspicious activity.

This is an area of preparedness that might not have been considered years back. It would've been standard practice. But people are seemingly getting more isolated. Many today aren't taking the time to get to know their neighbors as well as people did years ago.

I remember going to block parties every summer where neighbors would gather together, converse and enjoy each other's company. It came with the greater purpose of building greater community. Many today don't even know their next-door neighbors' names. Should a disaster strike, good relationships would pay big dividends. There would be any number of ways that neighbors could provide mutual benefits. It's worth meeting, chatting and having a cookout or two during the summertime.

Those who are talking to their neighbors might tastefully breach the topic of preparedness before any time of trouble strikes. You could find out what, if anything, the neighbors are doing to assure safety. You could share some of the household planning and determine any ways in which families in the neighborhood could cooperate for the greater good during a recovery process.

You might consider reaching out to a number of nearby homes. Though every neighborhood would have a good share of residents who aren't interested, a prepper might well find a number who have some similar thoughts or concerns. You might eventually come to meet once a month, once a season or once a year to talk about the state of the neighborhood and share in some planning discussion. It might not happen. All the same, there's nothing wasted in honest, friendly, well-intentioned talk with those equally invested in the wellbeing of your small, shared area.

Planning for a solid home recovery interestingly requires a number of thoughts that extend beyond the confines of its four walls. It takes a combination of big efforts and many smaller tasks to make any sized disaster more bearable on your family. It takes a lot of good, honest thought.

Home is our most treasured place. The home might be disheveled after a storm blows through. It might be chaotic. Challenges might well test the patience and emotions of even the strongest men and women. It's why the work is so important before the storm.

Those who must rely on a good preparedness plan even through a long-term recovery period would still find another cliché applicable. It's a mess. It's a lot work. It makes for a lot of stress. But it's still "home sweet home."

Rather than stand in line for hours, the author would see this as a gas station. Get a siphon hose and learn how to use it.

3

MAKING A MOVE

This tent city that sprung up in Haiti after the 2010 earthquake is not the type of place where you would want your family to live after a disaster. Planning can help you avoid this.

In many cases, whether it's the tornado or snow emergency, the plan to shelter in place could range from the only option to one that makes the very best sense. There's something to be said for the ability to immediately get to the task of getting life back in order after a situation blows over. In other cases, our dangers — whether

natural or man-made — present far too much risk to buckle down and wait for calm. Sometimes, it's far preferable to pack up and hit the road.

Plans for evacuation are sometimes an underplayed component of preparedness. It's a real and important option that could become lost to your greater problem-solving efforts. Evacuation might very well offer the best way to provide for your family. In some cases and in some places, good information and a reasonable amount of time would allow your family to think, pack and move well before the storm arrives. Sometimes, the only way to fully assure safety is to watch the comfort of home disappear from the rearview mirror.

The potential need to evacuate takes nothing away from the importance of having a well-devised plan for a home-based recovery. Everyone should all have the right tools and supplies ready to go. A well-rounded plan, however, recognizes the stocked-up fortress isn't necessarily built to meet the first critical task when it's finally time to put your thoughts and efforts to work. Survival is always the first priority.

Those preparing for an evacuation should make advanced determinations of what they'd need and what they'd like to have along for the trip. You should plan out several options as potential destinations. Those who plan well would have everything that's vitally important in places that are easy to remember. Thinking through a potential

When there's adequate warning time before an approaching disaster, it's often best to escape to safety as quickly as possible.

evacuation well in advance would make it that much easier for the family to comfortably move without worry at the very drop of a dime.

Some emergencies wouldn't give the prepper's family any say in the matter. Law enforcement and emergency management officials often make evacuation decisions when major emergencies loom. Such orders often leave residents with very few moments to spare. Developing a plan and finishing all of the advance work necessary to complement it would place that family in a far stronger position to get ahead of the mess those orders often create.

Leaving isn't always an easy decision. It adds to the disruption families already face when disasters close in. You might recognize that leaving could mean life is far easier when compared against those who instead take a gamble in toughing out approaching havoc.

The first step is to take risks seriously. It's pretty clear that millions of people impacted by Superstorm Sandy in 2012 didn't have adequate respect for the destruction that nature can unleash. Many might have been naïve. It was certainly a storm unlike anything those on the East Coast had experienced before. What's interesting is that so many had a sense of shock when the winds died and the damage finally showed.

They never figured it could happen to them. Those people would have been well served to look at the history books. The world's forces can't be taken lightly. Mother Nature doesn't discriminate. She certainly doesn't bend around highly populated zones.

Millions were left without power. Millions certainly didn't think enough about all of the flooding, the deaths and the billions of dollars in damages. It's very clear in noting millions of people stuck around despite adequate warning of the devastation on its way. Some people can't believe something until they see it with their own eyes. You would be wiser to heed the words of the experts. Sometimes, it's better to get out.

Hurricane Katrina in 2005 is one of the best of examples in recent history of the importance of preparation at any level. The storm offered lessons for individuals and households. It spoke to local government needs and provided instruction on what an effective federal response would entail. It very clearly illustrated the wisdom of escaping to safety as quickly as possible before disaster strikes.

Katrina presented a quagmire in so many ways. Troubles mounted from the moment the winds and rains cleared. It could have been a far less tragic situation for so many in the Gulf Coast had they heeded warnings and fled before having to experience Katrina's wrath.

The path and severity of the approaching hurricane were known for a few days before Katrina finally tore through the Gulf Coast. Government officials understood the potential for levee breaks. Loui-siana and Mississippi officials took the initial steps to begin evacuation of threatened coastal areas two days before landfall. The potential for trouble on a human scale was recognized just as early. Officials were aware that many wouldn't evacuate and, in many cases, didn't

If you are trying to evacuate and your car is in 3 feet of water, it's probably too late.

have the means to do so.

Officials ordered the mandatory evacuation of New Orleans on the day before the hurricane's landfall. There were many who simply ignored the government's demand they leave. Louisiana Gov. Kathleen Blanco referred to it as "hurricane roulette." Having experienced any number of other hurricanes, too many people were willing to take on the risk of Katrina and hope it wouldn't be any different than the less significant disruptions of the past.

Katrina was indeed different.

The hurricane made its first landfall in southern Florida on Aug. 25 before entering the Gulf of Mexico. The storm intensified, having reached a Category 5 designation on the day before its second landfall along the Gulf Coast. Shelters opened across the region to accommodate those fleeing from the hurricane's path.

The Louisiana Superdome, home of the National Football League's New Orleans Saints, had previously been used as a shelter for those with special needs. Plans were again put in place for the stadium to serve that purpose. On the evening before landfall, in recognizing that so many residents ignored mandatory evacuation orders, the city opened the dome as a shelter of last resort for the general population.

Katrina made landfall in Louisiana at about 6 a.m. on Aug. 29, 2005 as a Category 3 storm with sustained winds topping 115 mph. Its fury lasted less than a day. Its impacts stretched far longer.

Scenes from the Superdome were among the key images used by the media to illustrate the sheer misery of those who remained amid the flooded destruction of New Orleans. There weren't sufficient preparations in place. Crews unloaded food and water prior to landfall but did so in expectation of its use only for the special needs population. The dome didn't have nearly enough for the more than 10,000 people who arrived before the storm in search of safety. Numbers swelled after the storm passed as others sought refuge from the floodwaters.

The Superdome's role as a mass shelter lasted only for a few days. It all the same provided a terrible way for people to live even over so

It could make far better sense to slowly and methodically get things ready to leave on your own terms prior to a disaster than to be forced out after one.

short of a period. There was no air conditioning to provide relief from the sweltering temperatures. There wasn't water or power, and sanitation quickly eroded.

At the same time, people were prevented from leaving due to the danger of surrounding floodwaters. Within days, officials declared the stadium uninhabitable. Efforts quickly mounted with an aim at evacuating the entire city. The Superdome was foremost on the priority list. Work began to move those sheltered in the dome to the other locales including the Astrodome in Houston.

No bit of history could better describe why preppers should maintain evacuation as a key option.

The many people who fled from the Gulf Coast in advance of Katrina most certainly had their challenges but none like those who couldn't leave or for some reason decided to take that huge risk. A decision to stick around when there's time and awareness of a pending disaster goes against the very reasons for preparing.

Preppers rely on the rule of threes because it's a simple tool that allows them to quickly gauge needs in their efforts to stay alive. In that sense, evacuation follows in the very spirit of the rule. You couldn't be more fortunate than to have a full day of advance notice that sustained 100-mph winds would slam into the community. It certainly beats the 14 minutes of warning time that tornadoes typically offer.

It's worth taking time in our place of everyday safety to consider the alternative. The hurricane situation provides a great example. Even the well prepared could suffer tremendously from one poor decision to stick it out.

Any collection of stay-in-place preparations wouldn't do a bit of good if they were washed away by floodwaters. You couldn't shelter in place if waters encroached on your home and rose right up to the rooftop. There isn't a tool in a prepper's collection that offers more to safety

If your plan is to leave, leave early. Do not wait until the last minute.

and his ability to recover than his own common sense.

Too many across our great nation lack that vital provision. History has shown there will always be a handful of stubborn people who are determined to hold their ground no matter how severe the situation. Unfortunately, Katrina wasn't the only recent disaster that left clear examples of the dangers faced by those who ignore the threats.

Hurricane Isaac in 2012 drew evacuation orders in low-lying areas across the Gulf Coast. The reasons were elementary. With wide swaths of land below sea level, it was reasonable to expect the storm surge and pounding rains would result in significant flooding. In many areas, those expectations ultimately came to pass.

It's counterintuitive that anyone in those low-lying areas would've stayed. Many did, and many experienced the consequences of their choices. It wasn't for a lack of warning. Hurricanes in this era no longer sneak up on communities. Stark, clear facts and plenty of history weren't enough to convince so many to get moving as trouble approached. It's beyond reason.

The end-to-end reports regarding Superstorm Sandy's potential were impossible to ignore, yet so many found a way. Satellite imagery of that massive storm should've been enough to put a scare into those living hundreds of miles away from the comfort of the Midwest. The storm's size while still a hurricane and spinning in the Atlantic Ocean was nearly that of the country's entire eastern coastline.

Sandy weakened to less than hurricane status before landfall, but the gigantic storm came in with enough power to climb right behind Katrina in terms of damage on a historical scale as far as weather events emerging from the Atlantic Ocean. About 200 people died. People had more than adequate time to move inland.

Hurricane Isaac, in particular, provides an excellent example of the dismissive attitudes so many people exhibit when in the face of true dangers. The Category 1 storm eerily made landfall on the Gulf Coast seven years to the day of Hurricane Katrina. Some, however, looked no further than its designation as a Category 1 storm as reason enough to ignore evacuation orders.

Many took the storm's designation to mean the nearing hurricane carried far less risk than that brought by Katrina seven years earlier. I wonder if those in our country could ever make that mistake again. Sandy, after all, was no longer a hurricane after she reached shore and brought far more wrath than all but one storm carrying that designation.

The apathetic mindset on the Gulf Coast was particularly striking when considering the 20-20 vision that accompanies hindsight. Someone living in the Gulf Coast couldn't have forgotten all the devastation and suffering that struck just seven years earlier. History, in some ways, repeated itself. Emergency workers were back in 2012 and hacking open rooftops to free residents trapped in their attics amid flood waters just as they did after Katrina.

The recent Gulf Coast hurricanes offer several lessons to consider. I would hope a key lesson could go without saying: emergency personnel wouldn't demand people leave their homes without a very good reason to do so. When those charged with public safety say it's time to go, the only proper response for a family is to load up, get out and do so as quickly as possible. There's no good explanation for anyone to put their lives at severe risk when advance warnings and demands for evacuation are publicized and well known.

Those who made ill-advised decisions to stay in place despite proper notice provide a cautionary tale. Mere survival provides the best reason to develop a solid evacuation plan, but it isn't the only one. Again, preppers would want to consider the wisdom of relying on others when they're better off to rely on themselves.

New Orleans was the worst-case scenario in many respects, and as such, provides some good points to ponder for those building preparedness plans. The rule of threes speaks to living, but it doesn't necessarily speak to quality of life. Those who had no option but the Superdome in post-Katrina New Orleans went through plenty of turmoil. It's tough to imagine the filth and stench. The heat and the crowding are also difficult to consider. Reports of crime were rampant. It was simply untenable.

Even smaller-scale emergency shelter situations after far less destructive events are far from ideal. You could generally expect they'd be clean. Those who rely on those shelters would have access to food, water and places to sleep. They'd be out of the cold or heat as the case might be. Despite all of that, it wouldn't be easy.

Shelters would certainly provide a better place to sleep than the hard, cold ground outdoors. It's still fair to wonder how many of those who could have fled from any pending storm came to second-guess the decision to stick around. You couldn't expect much comfort when sharing the air and an ever tight space with hundreds and potentially thousands of others. Planning provides people a means to do better.

This would be a bad time to start planning an evacuation.

Planning in advance

Any number of dangers could open up the need to leave. Disaster situations aren't solely brought from nature's power. Man-made risks should also be part of your thought process. Those who live in close proximity to nuclear power plants should have evacuation plans ready should a very rare, though highly dangerous, meltdown force a quick move.

It's a risk that's at play for quite a number of people across the United States. There are more than 100 licensed nuclear reactors in our country and almost 3 million people live within 10 miles of an operating reactor. Millions upon millions more live within a 50-mile radius that would still be subject to the risk of some level of radioactive contamination. The United States Nuclear Regulatory Commission has emergency planning zones established for areas within 10 and 50 miles around each nuclear plant that address varying dangers that come with different proximities to a potential emergency.

Preparations for those living in one of those 50-mile zones might include a visit to the sheriff's department. You might strike up a conversation with the county's emergency management director. Local authorities would have access to the detailed, local emergency planning that's built specific to each of the country's nuclear plants. That information could provide a far clearer picture of the potential risks at hand at varying distances to any given plant. It would give the family a clearer picture as to where and how far they should travel in the event of an emergency.

Those who don't have a nuclear plant in their region might all the same conduct a little bit of research on other man-made threats nearby their homes. Those risks might not be as substantial and life changing as nuclear meltdown but could require families to leave their home for a few days or longer all the same. Some might come to recognize there's a chemical plant in the community that could present a risk of danger in the potential for spills. Train cars along a nearby rail line might haul flammables or other hazardous chemicals and present significant risks in the event of fire or derailment. Plans grow stronger with a solid accounting of the potential risks that could come knocking.

Mother Nature will more frequently give people cause for evacuation. As far as hurricanes, she keeps a pretty regular schedule. It's extremely important for those living in areas prone for hurricanes to have evacuation plans in place knowing the possibility exists each and every year from June through November. There's an average of nearly 12 named storms per year originating in the Atlantic Ocean and an average of 1.7 make landfalls as hurricanes in the United States every year, according to the National Oceanic and Atmospheric Administration.

Wildfires give others cause for evacuation. The fires destroy property and scorch vast stretches of land every year. Plans that would allow for a rapid, yet well-thought-out move are critical for those living in or near wooded areas. Thousands of wildfires ignite annually whether by lightning strikes, careless campers or otherwise. Government reports show that wildfires burned through an average 3.5 million acres annually from 2001 through 2010. Unlike those in areas where hurricanes strike, those in wildfire zones aren't as likely to have quick or clear information that could serve as a good basis to make an early decision to evacuate. Often, homes considered safe from any specific fire could move to the high-risk side of the scale with just a quick shift in wind direction.

It isn't uncommon during wildfires for a family to get a knock on the door from authorities who give a dire warning and demand that they be gone in an hour. There are stories out there of families who made fortunate decisions to act with more haste than demanded by emergency workers. There are families out there who scrambled to gather what they could, hit the door within 45 minutes and had flames at the back bumpers of their cars as they sped away into the dark, black smoke and on toward safety.

Many substantial threats that touch the country with regularity show that families that have the best readiness plans are the same families that are ready to leave. Preppers would be wise to break down all of the little, potential stumbling blocks that could complicate a move just as they would in building contingencies for home. Families should have some locales in mind they're comfortable in reaching in each direction depending on the nature of their threats and the potential movement of those dangers, whether it's the hurricane's winds, rapidly moving flames or otherwise.

Preppers might build some advance knowledge of the places identified as potential getaways. Some might rely on the homes of family members. Some might be fortunate enough to own a little piece land several hours from the home that might have a cabin, or at least a place to pitch a tent.

If an uncle's home becomes a standby option and it's known he's allergic to dogs, it wouldn't hurt to have some contact information handy for boarding businesses in that region so you could make appropriate plans for pet care while the family is on the road. Those who consider camping as an option and don't have personal land to rely upon might want contact information for any number of campgrounds in the direction they're heading. It's worth noting that others affected by approaching turmoil could very well be thinking the same thing.

The only firm rule for evacuation is getting to a place far enough away to avoid danger. After that, it's a matter of personal choices that are largely dependent on your abilities and comfort. Some people might be comfortable living from their cars along roadsides, in parking lots or at rest stops for a couple of weeks with a small collection of gear. Another family's evacuation plan might call for a six- to eight-hour drive to a nice hotel with a big swimming pool. That's also a suitable option, so long as the family has the financial means to turn tough times into a well-deserved vacation. The important thing is to have a plan assembled before the emergency calls for action. It's a matter of being able to move efficiently and comfortably. Time is always of the essence.

Having multiple destinations laid out through evacuation planning is important in recognizing the unpredictability of disaster events. Those at risk should be able to wisely choose a route that assures they're legitimately out of harm's way. Adding depth provides less to think about when times get

Those in areas that are prone to wildfires should take the proper steps to protect their property well in advance of a blaze risk.

tough. Those planning might do so in the same fashion they'd map out a vacation. Few people get in their cars for the family trip without a game plan or any idea of what to expect upon reaching their destinations. Having some options laid out that go beyond a mere dot on the highway map eliminates one more area of stress.

Those at risk for wildfires have it simple. The move is simply a matter of getting clear from those dry, wooded zones at risk of burning into a clear and lush locale. Approaching hurricanes can provide for a little more difficulty. It isn't possible to make any precise predictions as to where storms will strike or how far their damages would spread.

The favorite of your several evacuation options might not always be the best option for any specific threat. Those at risk should look at all of the best information available and choose accordingly. Those who live along the East Coast and have evacuation options in place for any number of risks are far more limited by hurricanes. The best and only safe place to head is inland. It isn't uncommon for hurricanes to move along lengthy stretches of coastline. Sandy caused problems from Florida clear to Maine.

Those with homes in Florida best illustrate that some evacuation plans require more thought

than others. The peninsula hangs out there in the midst of many hurricanes' paths. Consider the hypothetical hurricane threatening those on Florida's east coast. Inland travel might not offer much for a guarantee.

Those folks might instead move northwest in a fashion in which they're driving at an angle away from the oncoming storm. They'd be wise to pay close attention to the latest news while traveling should the storm path require some late improvisation. Again, it's a matter of thinking through all the smaller problems that develop from a bigger issue.

The importance of thinking through the right locales for evacuation was illustrated during the tumultuous hurricane season of 2005. A number of evacuees displaced by Hurricane Katrina were moved west and housed in an arena in Lake Charles, La. It's near the Texas border and not far from the coast. In less than a month, Hurricane Rita came up through the Gulf of Mexico and forced those people to pick up and move for a second time.

We refer to our practice as preparation for a reason. Comfort tomorrow might well depend on the work finished today. The worst possible time for anyone to start thinking about a move is when the authorities order the neighborhood to go.

Families that include young children or pets will have a few more contingencies to think about during their planning efforts. Those who have infants, for example, might keep a spare, unopened can of formula set aside and at easy reach. Those with older children might plan to have some easy-to-pack games, books and puzzles to break the boredom and offer some comfort. Evacuation is a stressful endeavor for the little ones just as it is for their parents.

Most pet owners consider their companions as far more than animals. They're members of the family, and as such, preppers should have what's needed to make sure their dogs and cats — or whatever those friends might be — can come along for the ride. One of the sadder sights during my efforts in Hurricane Katrina's wake were the dogs tied up in backyards when it was clear their owners went off in search of safety. Our pets provide one more reason to adequately think ahead.

Owners wouldn't be wise to keep pet food stored away in the vehicle. Mice or other vermin don't need that welcome invitation. It would make sense, however, for pet owners to assure the food supply doesn't get below the level needed for at least several days of feeding. It's a contingency that makes just as much sense for the home-based recovery plan. Pet owners thinking about the need to leave should always have enough to grab for the get-away.

Those planning for evacuation should recognize their contingencies aren't a matter of accounting for the long term. The car or minivan isn't going to hold a three-month supply of anything and doesn't need to serve that purpose.

Wildfires are relentless and fast. In the aftermath, there's often not much left to salvage.

It's a matter of having enough to get wherever it is that you are going. Upon reaching places of safety, those who evacuated will be able to get to a store and pick up whatever items are necessary to replenish supplies.

Beyond safety, those planning should think from the perspective of limiting the emotional distress an emergency situation could bring to your life. It's also a matter of setting some clear priorities. Whether it's flooding or a fire, no one can pack up every last bit of his belongings before setting out.

People can, however, carry along their most cherished pieces. Preppers should think about the small and lightweight items they might tuck away for the ride with an ultimate focus on what's most

meaningful. Those planning for evacuation should consider the real possibility of returning from an event and finding nothing left.

Furniture, clothing, vehicles and all types of household goods can be replaced. Those forced from their homes, however, aren't going to replace those heirloom pieces of jewelry that were handed down in the family from generation to generation. Should flooding or a fire strike, no insurance company could restore the children's first-grade school pictures or Dad's collection of World War II medals.

It's an interesting exercise to go through the home and determine those items that truly mean the most. It's also an important one. Families should keep those small, important items in a safe where they're protected every day and easy to grab when a situation requires a quick move.

Preppers should assemble a checklist so they're not struggling to remember every last thing amid the stress of that ticking clock. You should keep a storage bin or some other means of collection at the ready for quick packing of those irreplaceable goods whether it's a few photo albums, jewelry or any number of documents.

I keep a loose-leaf binder in my safe containing clear, plastic pages in which I can store any number of those irreplaceable certificates,

awards and other pieces of my story. For many, high school or university diplomas aren't hanging on display. They're nonetheless important recognitions, pieces of our histories and items that folks would feel terrible about losing to a disaster. I keep another binder containing other important documents ranging from vehicle titles and mortgage papers to life insurance policies and passports.

Preppers might keep a notebook in the safe or elsewhere that's in easy reach in the event of evacuation that includes contact information for everyone they owe money to or otherwise engage in business. The notebook might include account numbers in addition to phone numbers. It's a small step that could make life that much easier when away.

Certainly, the power company

Digital storage is inexpensive. Portable hard drives that can store up to 1 terabyte are reasonably priced. Back up your files.

and mortgage company would have the ability to look up your account information, but that bit of preparation is going to make things more convenient. The notebook would serve as a reference that would eliminate any concerns about forgetting something important. Any bit of efficiency that's put in place beforehand is going to go a long way to providing some ease amid difficulty.

Electronic files might very well fall among your irreplaceable items in this digital world. In an evacuation, those who work from laptops could easily grab their computers before fleeing. Those who own desktop computers might not do the same. People should back up their files. Digital storage is inexpensive and grows cheaper by the year. It's a good idea, whether for laptop or desktop, at any point and for reasons well beyond the chance of disaster.

Technology could also have a hand in protecting other items of personal value. Preppers might invest in a decent photo scanner. They're fairly inexpensive and good investments from the standpoint of emotional well-being. Photos are crucial pieces of our families' stories.

In the event of any disaster, whether it's hurricane-related flooding, a wildfire or even the typical house fire, scanned images would provide one less cause for stress, worry or mourning. Certainly, it's not the same to have a digital file as that original picture of your great grandmother on century-old photo paper, but something is always better than nothing.

You might store the images on CDs, DVDs or a flash drive. Some people have cloud-based accounts. It would make sense to send copies to other family members or put copies in the safe deposit box. Any of those options would provide yet one more assurance those photos are always safe and available regardless of what this unpredictable world could bring.

It's smart to keep some cash in a safe that isn't touched and there for the taking in the event of an evacuation. It's really up to each person as to how much he is able to put away and how much he would feel comfortable carrying. It would make sense to have $100 available for each member of the family. It's a contingency that recognizes credit cards aren't foolproof. In the midst of emergencies, you might find businesses that are able to keep their doors open but lost the computers and can't make credit card transactions. Every business takes cash.

When disasters approach

Families would be wise to use the full extent of their advance notice when solid information of pending disaster becomes available. Last-minute decisions and orders forced by authorities create new difficulties for those in their attempts to get out of harm's way. Heavy outbound traffic could stifle a clean getaway. It makes the best sense to leave before many have the same inclination, whether those evacuations are forced or not.

Having solid evacuation contingencies at the ready would mean little for those who don't have vehicles that are in proper shape to whisk them away from oncoming danger. Of course, everyone would be in a far better place with the big, ultimate "bug out vehicle." A big, old Chevy Suburban or other SUV with the large, wide tires and huge gas tank would provide comfort and assurance and basically serve as a shelter on wheels. Most, however, just have to do the best with what's sitting in the driveway.

Those evacuating should load in their go-bags — often called three-day emergency kits — as a contingency plan should they encounter any problems while on the road. A well-assembled bag will have a number of provisions including a first-aid kit, some ways to start a fire, some food and water and means to replenish. It'll carry some basic tools. Bags often include a small tent. It's a bag built to meet the rule of threes for three days.

Many keep a cache of survival gear

The author recommends always scanning or making copies of your credentials. Besides keeping them digitally, he also keeps a printed version hidden.

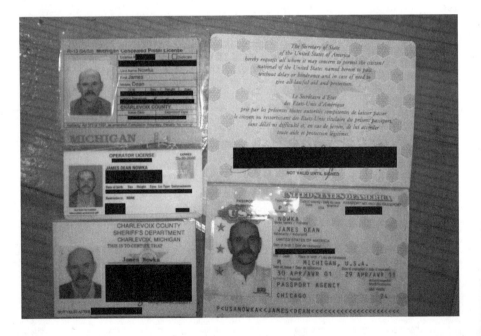

packed away in their vehicles. It's a good idea. I have a vinyl foot locker on my Jeep loaded up with a number of items that would afford the means to set up a camp if ever needed. The kit contains some silicone tarps. There's a hatchet. The box holds a set of wrenches and a ratchet and sockets among a small cache of tools should repairs become necessary.

It would be optimal to have a vehicle that has every last thing you would ever need ready to go at a moment's notice. That, too, isn't possible. Given heat degradation, you certainly wouldn't want to keep food provisions packed in a trunk for any period of time. Most families in most situations would do perfectly well in running down a well-devised checklist before loading up and heading out.

Vehicle readiness is just another matter of exercising common sense. Preppers should always keep the gas tank topped off. It's a little, everyday thing that many people fail to think about. It's among the smallest pieces of the preparedness puzzle and could pretty quickly become a matter of habit for most people.

From a position of preparedness, it's frightening to consider the many who only think about pulling into the gas station when the "low fuel" light finally starts to brighten up on their dashboards. It isn't a big deal on the average day. Most people are always in pretty close proximity to a gas station or two.

Don't forget your pets and their needs when making your disaster plans.

Having only a quarter-full gas tank or less could become a really big issue for people should emergencies force quick evacuations. Those forced from their homes would quickly learn many others were forced out alongside them. It's not uncommon after evacuation orders to find lengthy lines at each and every gas station.

Moments of high and immediate demand could open a risk of short-

A wall tent is perfect for setting up house during the recovery phase of a disaster.

Preparation calls for the right tools to meet the right situations. There is not one perfect tent to carry a family through all of its potential needs. Any family should look at a couple of tents with the aims of fulfilling short-term survival situations and the potential need for longer-term housing.

In each case, think about durability and ease in set-up. A survival situation isn't the time to fumble with instructions. For that matter, you wouldn't want to compromise your efforts by snapping off one of those flimsy fiberglass poles. In the longer term, durability is an obvious consideration. Ease also has an important place. A disaster is going to mean there are a variety of tasks to accomplish, and you would do well for yourself in getting that shelter up as a base of operations as quickly as possible.

When choosing a tent for the go-bag, go for something that's small and light. The tent is only one part of a bigger package,

and the entire pack has to be carried. That tent will be less about usual comforts than it is a means of keeping out of the elements. Backpacking tents work well for those sleeping one or two. Those who are bugging out as a family could find some pretty large dome tents that pack up fairly small and can sleep four to eight people.

Those purchasing a tent that could serve as home after disaster might go for something substantial. A number of tents could offer a touch of comfort in a difficult spot. You might set up camp right at the remnants of the house to allow for prompt and efficient work. Montana Canvas, for instance, makes a 10-by-12 wedge tent that feels more like a room inside. You could put a wood stove in there. If it's 20 degrees below zero beyond the canvas walls, you could easily bring it to a comfortable 60 degrees inside.

Some of the cabin tents out there are pretty incredible and good options to consider. There are a number of durable, canvas models on the market. Some people actually put floors inside and use them as vacation homes.

Those preparing for the destructive events that might require alternative shelter on their properties might consider stepping beyond what most typically think of as tents. The portable garages out there are typically 10-by-20 feet. It's a lot of space. One or two of those shelters would allow a family to set up some kitchen and dining room space as well as a couple bedrooms. You might put some air conditioners in there. It wouldn't be the house. It might still feel like home.

Choose according to the family's needs. There isn't a tent that's going to feel as comfortable as the house. In the midst of crisis, the closer you can get, the easier the recovery process will be to manage.

(above) There are no tents that will be as comfortable for your family as your house, but some tents come complete with amenities like a front door.

(right) Wall tents are durable and comfortable in most environments.

age. Empty gas tanks at that point could ruin the chances of some to get out from the approaching threat. It's an unenviable position.

Low gas tanks might seem like a little thing. Well-built plans are stacked brick by brick from the little things. One missing brick weakens the entire structure. Those who exercised appropriate forethought could pull onto the highway on-ramp with some sense of relief while peering down at the long lines at the pumps of the adjacent gas station. It pays to think ahead.

Preppers should keep their vehicles well maintained. It's important to keep up on the regular oil changes. It's wise to have well-conditioned, properly inflated tires. Owning a vehicle that's ready to go in an evacuation scenario is really just a matter of following through on all the safety and maintenance considerations that are just as important on the typical day.

Preparing the home is also important. The best means of doing so, however, are accomplished long before the emergency that's going to force your family's flight. Those in hurricane zones should have shutters installed. They can quickly be closed up and locked before the family gets on the road. Those who haven't gone that far should at least have pre-cut plywood that can quickly be tacked up over the windows. Any family could run through that same set of thoughts applicable at vacation time. Make sure the oven is off. Lock the doors. Hope for the best. After all of that, it's time to get moving.

Those in wildfire zones who fail to take the proper steps to protect their property well in advance of a blaze risk having everything they've worked for reduced to ash. Wildfires are relentless. Preparing the home for wildfires, meanwhile, isn't something that can be accomplished in a quick manner when the threat is bearing down.

The homes at highest risk are those built in the woods or those with wild growth coming right up to the front doors. You could understand how those with a strong appreciation for nature and all of its beauty want their homes surrounded by that wonder. It's still quite the gamble.

Those living near wooded areas should clear away the underbrush on their property and keep the home some distance from the greater area at risk of burning. It's wise to consider some type of fire suppression system. There are means on the market that would allow you to keep water spraying on the house should a wildfire encroach. Those living amid wildfire risk should have homes built with fire-resistant materials.

Those who prepare well can do a

lot to limit how much a disaster can take away. Firefighters who work in wildfire zones are tremendously well trained, but it's up to those homeowners to give them a fighting chance. Too often, they have their work cut out for them.

It's a pretty good concession for homeowners to keep a reasonable buffer between their homes and the nature they love. The firefighters want to save those homes. They often arrive in losing positions.

In many ways, a life of preparation is a life of paying attention. A decision on whether to leave is a personal one that should take several factors into account, but you shouldn't necessarily rely on an emergency management authority to declare the order. There's no harm done by getting out of the way in figuring it's better to be safe than sorry.

Those who live in homes below sea level would be wise to weigh safety far and beyond any thoughts of comfort. It's not a matter of if water will find its way into the home. It's a matter of when. Katrina provided a devastating demonstration. Isaac offered a second reminder.

Those who live in close vicinity to active wildfires might show some vigilance. It could make far better sense to slowly and methodically get things ready and leave on your own terms. Families can do better for themselves than have to scramble amid a one-hour notice.

Families far too often lack notice of pending destruction. Those who have the power of advanced warning are fortunate. Evacuation isn't an easy decision. You could reach a good decision quickly by thinking through all you stand to gain and all you stand to lose by sticking around.

Preppers always turn back to the rule of threes. Families who make it a few hundred miles away from the danger zone would have access to food, water and shelter without much struggle in attaining it. Those who choose to stay in place despite significant warning are in many cases making a decision that's akin to marooning the family on an island.

The gas pumps aren't pumping when the power is out. Highways might close down due to structural damage. Those folks within whatever zone of destruction could be stuck there for quite some time.

It's wise to make a good decision early. Those who choose to stick around might no longer have the ability to change their minds after the disaster is gone and its aftermath is underway. If you didn't exercise appropriate forethought, you might have a tougher time of things when finally recognizing life is far easier just a short trek up the highway.

4

FOOD

A cellar such as this one would serve as a good a storage place as long as it's dry.

Food planning and storage when considered from the place of preparation provides another interesting example of how much society has changed over only the last half century or so. It's a topic that those new to prepping might find is a pretty big departure from their everyday lifestyles. Really, though, the idea of having

a good amount of food on hand to ensure the family could account for their long-term needs is nothing new.

Many of the efforts taken on by preppers today to ensure the family would have enough to eat after disaster were matters of everyday course just a few generations back.

A well-stocked pantry will get you through most natural disasters until help arrives or things get back to normal.

Until very recent times, food took far more thought and effort even for the short term. It wasn't so far back when having just a week's worth of food at hand might well have caused families some pretty deep worries.

A week's worth of groceries is the norm today. More options exist now than did then. We do have things easier, though it's just as wise to think ahead today as it's always been. Should disaster strike, the family that is ready and has a good supply of food in the home is going to be far more comfortable than the family that's hoping for and waiting for help with no good assurances.

Believe it or not, many still live with a long-term sensibility as it comes to food. Preppers, among many others, will plant extensive gardens and do some canning at harvest time just as their forefathers did. These are good skills to have and make for some great meals. It's a practice that's never disappeared among those in the rural areas of our country.

Hunters, if they're fortunate when in the field, always have a good supply of game stored away in the freezer. It provides for meals throughout the year and until the next season arrives. It's the way people had always lived.

Modern technology has made long-term preparation far easier than what it was for our grandparents. Some preppers, whether for lack of a space, ability or interest in utilizing the more old-school methods of food stocking, will rely heavily — sometimes exclusively — on shelf-stable products that are available commercially. Factory canned foods, freeze-dried foods, dried grains and other goods remain viable for years and often decades. They allow for the family to eat well and without worry should a disaster send the greater community into panic as the grocery stores start to empty out.

Planning to those levels might sound strange to those who've never known anything else but fulfilling their grocery lists on a weekly basis. It's more a function of our society's short memory. Long-term food storage goes back to the earliest history of human civilization. Technology has simplified the day-to-day, but it's come at the deep cost of readiness for the unforeseeable. The change in how American society views food has been as dramatic as it's been quick.

Food for many in the modern era has become an afterthought. It's a grab-and-go society. You eat when you're hungry, and you don't have to put forth much effort to scrounge up a meal. The drive-through down the road is often viewed as an inexpensive and reliable standby when time runs thin or groceries run low. Fast food places are rarely more than a few minutes from any home in urban and suburban environments. Today, there are more than 160,000 of them across the country.

That all-too-common relationship with food would open the door to some serious troubles upon disaster. Those whose meal-time plans and habits run no deeper than restaurant trips and keeping a few staples in their kitchens are setting themselves up for hunger should emergencies occur. Our grocery stores, ironically like most of the people they serve, don't stock up their goods for the long-term. Store shelves can go bare pretty quickly when disasters or even the panic brought on by short-term emergencies impact a community.

History has shown that preppers aren't dealing with the undocumented and hypothetical when it comes to planning for food on a long-term basis even in our modern era. Stores actually do empty out. I saw it in Haiti. It happened after Katrina. It happens even in events on a far smaller scale. Those new to prepping might start with some thoughts of spending even a few uncomfortable days without a decent meal.

In 2010, a number of grocery stores in New York City went empty and were barren for several days after December blizzard conditions gave street crews more than they could hastily handle. Grocery stores typically replenish supplies as they sell and rely on a continuing stream of deliveries to keep their shelves stocked. Drivers were unable to get through the snow to make their regular deliveries. Customers cleared the grocery stores out, and those who came by too late were left wondering what they'd do in the meantime.

One might think about the vulnerabilities that exist among their available resources. A destructive 2011 tornado in tiny Leakesville, Miss., illustrated the wisdom of having a sufficient amount of food in the home as insurance against the unpredictable. The community

of just more than 1,000 people had its troubles compounded when the storm caused significant damage to its only grocery store and the only one for miles around.

The recovery period was marked with some impatience and frustration. Food became a real issue for many residents there. Families faced with rebuilding also looked at lengthy drives to restock their own shelves as local storeowners awaited the repairs needed before they could safely reopen their doors.

Major disasters stand to impact food availability to some extent over the long-term. Hurricane Katrina's impact on New Orleans continued well after clean-up was complete. The food crisis went beyond the closure of stores just prior to and through the storm's immediate aftermath in 2005. Many neighborhoods were impacted well beyond by the decisions of storeowners to keep their doors shuttered.

As of January 2009, only 19 full-service supermarkets had reopened in the city. It was about half the number of supermarkets that operated in New Orleans before Katrina. The business decisions were more damaging than some might think given the sizable numbers of people in that city that don't have vehicles. Fresh, healthy, decent foods weren't so easy for many of the lower income people in the city to acquire.

Accounting for food needs in the wake of disaster requires a shift away from the modern-day, common approach to eating. Many people take food for granted, and during any usual day, it isn't so difficult to understand why. Preparing requires a step back to the vigilance that food demanded from those in days gone by. You can and should enjoy the wonders of modern convenience. The dangers start to settle in when people begin to lean too heavily on all of the ease it offers.

After a disaster, grocery store shelves will usually not look like this. They go bare pretty quickly because the stores do not stock for the long-term.

Think back to your own childhood. The younger folks can ask your parents or grandparents. Cooking wasn't considered as a hobby or interest back then as it often is today. It was a daily necessity.

Speed and ease truly have become the top priorities of society at large. Believe it or not, people went to gas stations decades back with few intentions beyond filling up their gas tanks and maybe getting the windshield wiper fluid topped off. They weren't confronted with sprawling spaces loaded up with ready-to-grab junk foods. Today, some are more likely to have a meal from behind their steering wheel than they are from the dining room table.

Those new to prepping should take inventory of their eating habits to get a better sense of what you need to accomplish. You might quickly recognize how your own attitudes stack up with preparedness goals with a quick look at the food supply. You should ask yourself whether you could make it for a few weeks or even longer without restaurants, gas stations or trips to the grocery store. Those who could answer affirmatively have great head starts. Far too many couldn't.

Everyone should at the very least have enough food at hand to provide for all of the family's needs for a few weeks. If a huge storm rolled in and a major, widespread power outage struck, the grocery store might no longer be an option. Further, the fast food joints couldn't power their grills and the pizza delivery guys wouldn't be there to pick up the phones.

Life is different during a disaster. It's difficult to imagine for many of those who haven't expe-

rienced those hardships. Preppers would just as soon avoid those pitfalls. There are many who prep who keep enough food in storage to manage for several months in the interest of keeping safely ahead of any potential dangers. Some think even further beyond.

Those who live in an area apt for a tornado might think about all of the things that could change in a matter of minutes. You could expect to go without power for some time. You could certainly expect the businesses that you relied upon for short-term food purchases to close down to handle their own damages.

Like so

It does not take much to put aside a little extra each week to stock a pantry.

many areas of preparation, it all comes back to your mindset. You wouldn't have to step back that far into history to get a sense of what food planning required before our current era. The regular efforts of decades back would put today's families in far better position to comfortably manage through an emergency.

Change did come quickly. It's interesting to note that only a quarter of U.S. households had microwaves as late as 1986. Today, virtually everyone has the appliance, and thus, the ability to warm a TV dinner from frozen in a couple minutes. A prepper might recognize it's nothing more than a metal box without a power supply.

The older folks among us would vividly remember how different things used to be in their younger days when it came to feeding the family. Certainly, well-planned, home-cooked meals were far more the norm back then. They ate balanced meals. They ate slower and recognized their dinner hours as important times to bond as a family. The shift, however, goes beyond those warm thoughts of good food and better company around the big dining room table.

People thought ahead. Mothers and grandmothers didn't have to scramble moments before the dinner hour to cobble a quick meal together. They rarely had to make those last-second trips for ingredients before assembling those memorable, dinnertime masterpieces. They certainly didn't have to do their best with the last few goods in the pantry or freezer in recognizing that shopping day was still a day or two out.

Families back then always had significant amounts of food stored away. Further, they didn't think anything of having a sizable supply at reach. Their neighbors did the same. They stored as a matter of practice because self-reliance was the only reliance they had.

Certainly, life was different in a variety of respects. People years

ago relied more on their land than people do today. Eating during the winter required many people to store away sufficient food during the growing season. It wasn't called prepping. It didn't have a name. It was simply a matter of getting by.

It's fair to say that today's generation is spoiled when stacked against those of yesteryear. The grocery store of just a few decades ago looked far different than the sprawling supermarkets that typify the shopping experience of today.

Remember, the food you store is the stuff that will keep your energy up and your stomach full when a disaster strikes. Stock your pantry accordingly.

The grocery store of a century ago might be unrecognizable as such to younger folks. Back then, they were the corner shops carrying little more than the basic staples such as flour or sugar and a limited selection of canned or otherwise pre-packaged goods.

People ate differently. The family that had fresh meat on the table was the family in which the men just came home from a successful hunt. The remainder of the meat was cured and stored away.

The ability to purchase large varieties of fresh fruits and vegetables on a year-round basis would've been the mark of an overactive imagination for our grandparents. It's interesting to think about how so many today couldn't imagine anything different. Years ago, the country lacked any reliable and economical means to get fresh foods into the stores to the level expected by today's consumers.

The youngest out there might have difficulty in grasping that you couldn't always pull a few bucks out of your wallet for a bunch or two of still-green bananas. Even 30 or 40 years ago, stores didn't have much for fresh produce sections. The idea of picking up a carton of fresh, ripe cherry tomatoes during the deep freeze of winter in our grandparents' era was beyond consideration. It would have been laughable.

Life wasn't as simple back then, but it forced people to rely on themselves. They did what it took to get by, and they were far better prepared because of it. Those who wanted to eat fresh were more likely to rely on their own produce, and of course, only during the growing season. Those who wanted ripe, juicy apples picked them from their own trees or were given a bag from friends or neighbors. Those who enjoyed grapes grew their own vines.

People traded produce with their neighbors in an effort to increase their variety. Many would go to farm markets. They preserved what was left over to account for the cold weather months.

Prepping from a food perspective in this era of convenience, variety and abundance isn't as primitive as some might think. There are a growing number of people today extolling the virtues of diets rich in locally grown produce. Growing numbers are recognizing the unhealthy aspects of convenience eating. Farm markets, though long popular, are starting to see some new customers.

Some view preparedness as some kind of new trend. Honestly, there's nothing new about it. So many of the things preppers need to consider to assure family safety after a disaster, whether it's food or otherwise, are more a matter of re-membering life as it used to be. The idea of having a strong food supply in the home never lost importance. Most, however, simply failed to recognize it.

Getting started

Getting a good start on food planning requires some thought on the length of time the family would want to be able to meet from a place of self-reliance. Some are comfortable with an emergency food supply that would feed the family for a month. Others will assemble and stock a food locker that accounts for three months of meals. Smaller numbers aren't comfortable in taking any chances and have an emergency supply that would sustain the family for a year or more.

There isn't an overall right or wrong answer. Risks vary across the country. Even those living in the same region would have varying degrees of comfort. You might hold lesser confidence than another in the ability of society-at-large to restore food supplies with certain haste. A few out there want to be ready for doomsday. Everyone is different.

The frequency of short- to mid-term emergencies suggests real risk in having any less than several weeks of food ready to go at any given time. After meeting that minimum, you should build your storage locker according to your own concerns. It's a process that should be undertaken with some reason. You shouldn't have to over-extend the family finances to reach your desired threshold.

Many preppers would suggest that having a food locker that would cover a few months is pretty reasonable. Major disasters have certainly impacted community food supplies for extended periods. The family with the food locker built for a month or less could run the risk of depleting supplies too quickly after highly destructive events.

On the other end, some would argue food plans that extend beyond a year serve only to delay the inevitable if something should happen that would require use of that full supply. If stores are gone for that long, you might surmise they aren't coming back. At and before that point, you would want to look to planting and hunting or potentially raising animals for sustenance just as people did in the old days.

The next big question to ponder is how much food you would need for the family to eat. Those prepping should take note of what the family is eating in the day-to-day when planning their stock to meet their chosen timeframes. Pay attention to typical consumption and then purchase enough that would allow family members to ratchet up caloric intake as needed during a period of recovery. Your typical diet might not be sufficient based on the stresses and physical requirements bound to accompany a disaster aftermath.

The U.S. Department of Agriculture's recommendations for caloric intake differ not only by age and sex but also by one's level of activity. An average, sedentary 40-year-old man, for instance, would need 2,400 calories to balance his intake with the energy his body would burn as a matter of living. The same man, if active, would need 2,800 calories to meet the needs of body function and that added exertion.

Women typically require less food than men to account for what their bodies burn. The average, sedentary 40-year-old woman would need 1,800 calories, according to the USDA. Her active counterpart would require 2,200 to maintain a healthy balance. Caloric needs tend to peak for men and women as they move through their late teens and early 20s. Active men in their 20s to mid-30s typically require 3,000 calories a day while their female counterparts would need about 2,400.

Those planning for food storage to account for a disaster should aim for the higher end of the calorie charts for several reasons. It'll take more than light meals — salads wouldn't suffice — to properly fuel the body when putting forth some heavy labor that isn't part of your normal routine. Recovery takes real work. Even the in-shape prepper who spends 40 minutes a day at the gym would likely encounter some pretty big demands on the body depending on the extent of any damage left behind in a disaster event.

Following a disaster, you'd have to deal not only with exertion but also with working the body in ways in which it isn't accustomed. You might be stressing muscles that don't get much work on the average day. There might be trees to chop and wood to haul. It's possible you'd tackle some of your own roofing work or repair on other damages left to the family home.

Your energy output might well extend beyond muscular considerations depending on circumstances. Winter emergencies could put families in situations of limited heat. If the furnace went out, it might well mean hunkering down in 50-degree temperatures rather than the more comfortable 70 degrees. In that circumstance, the body would burn some additional calories in its own efforts to maintain sufficient warmth.

MREs, a common pack-away for preppers, tend to suggest that calorie intake for the common day and the average man or woman wouldn't suffice for the highly ac-

tive. The meals are designed for soldiers and used by the military but are readily available to the civilian community. Each comes at more than 1,200 calories. It goes without saying that the sedentary man or woman wouldn't want to have three per day for any length of time if he or she is looking to maintain a slender waistline.

Those planning their food stock should just as much rely on logic and good sense in planning out amounts that go beyond the usual. The very point of storage is to make it through any period that would present an inability to replenish the shelves. It's a far better position to recognize you might have over-prepared than it is to watch food supplies dwindle when the community still hasn't recovered.

Thoughts would turn from how much food is sufficient to what types of foods would best leave the family ready for whatever a disaster might bring. Assembling your food for the long-term has some elements that aren't all that different from how you go about your grocery shopping on a week in and week out basis. Whether you are planning for next week or for food to last for an entire year, you're still going to think about how to provide for some variety and decent, balanced meals and snacks. The body's need for good nutrition doesn't halt when a disaster happens. Good

MREs, or Meals Ready to Eat, are an easy long-term solution for a prepper's meal planning.

plans will include fruits, vegetables, grains and protein sources.

There's one key difference when buying for the long term. You have to pay attention to how long those foods would survive on the shelf. Your potential food selections become far narrower. The deli, produce and bakery sections of the store aren't going to do much for the long-term shopper. "Use by" dates take on a far greater level of importance. It requires some good strategy.

It's vital to have enough food. It's just as vital to have the right food. Many people have chest freezers in the basement. They're great appliances from the perspective of extending the family's food supplies. You shouldn't, however, consider those frozen food items as part of your long-term emergency provisions.

The basement freezer would certainly stand to provide for the family's needs pretty well in the very shortest of terms. In a case of electricity loss, the freezer would become the immediate priority of your meal planning. The family would have to get through as much as possible before its contents thawed and became spoiled.

Preppers buying for the long-term have to think differently, but there are nonetheless many options available that would allow a person to eat pretty well. You wouldn't have to survive only on rice and water. The numbers of foods that'll hold up for the long term are becoming more plentiful all the time.

There are many different ways to tackle a suitable food plan. Those looking for the ultimate in convenience could achieve everything needed to feed the family for an entire year without stepping off of their properties. It could be as simple as pulling out the credit card, spending 10 minutes on the Internet and waiting for the delivery truck to arrive.

A variety of companies offer annual packs of freeze-dried and canned foods with shelf lives of 25 years or more. They're specifically assembled to offer some variety and take away the guess-work in building a preparedness plan. It's a viable option for some people, though it isn't difficult to imagine the price factor would drive many toward other options.

The packages start at about $1,000 and can go to $3,000 or beyond. The packages, meanwhile, are usually put together on a per-person basis. Many of the packages out on the market aren't unreasonable from a cost perspective when broken down to a per-meal basis.

MREs are highly mobile. Everything you need in order to heat and eat them is included.

Some are comparable to how much people would spend on food for the family from week to week.

What becomes unreasonable for many is the idea of building a full year of additional food that'll be stashed away, lying in wait and paid for in one, big, lone transaction. It wouldn't work for a lot of people's budgets. Whether it's planning a home improvement or saving for the next car, the average family of four wouldn't likely have $4,000 to $12,000 in rainy day money to spend on that kind of insurance regardless of how important they find it.

A family could build a good degree of security with methods that are a little bit friendlier to the pocketbook. Food plans, like so many areas of preparation, can be developed gradually. The family that doesn't have a lot of expendable cash can still set a solid plan into action bit by bit. A food plan might not stretch to a year or even several months of contingency right from the get-go. A new prepper might recognize that simply beginning your plan puts your family in a far stronger position than most.

Your family might start by doubling up on the typical grocery bill when a little extra money becomes available. You could load up a second cartload and get the pantry stocked sufficiently to meet a couple of weeks' worth of meals instead of just one. You might then build on that by adding a few additional shelf-stable, long-viable products to the cart during each subsequent shopping trip.

Much of your plans wouldn't necessarily require any firm line of separation between your preps and your family's everyday eating. The important part of preparation is getting that solid foundation laid so your family's food availability stretches beyond the immediate. A number of items — based on shelf life — might rotate from the emergency food locker to the everyday pantry when you shop and bring home some replacements.

After that foundation is in place and your family has a sizable cache of food, you might grab a new can of sweet corn from the grocery store based on Sunday's recipe. You could then swap it out for the can that's been in the locker for six months or a year and is still well beneath its "best by" date. That Sunday meal wouldn't taste a bit different. The family, meanwhile, could maintain an emergency locker of fairly recent goods.

Many foods that a family would typically purchase for their day-to-day living would hold up perfectly well for several years. Canned goods are a great example. The canning process entails the use of high heat to kill off bacteria in food and establishing a vacuum seal to prevent new bacteria from getting in. The bacteria are what cause food to spoil.

Many commercially canned goods remain viable for lengthy periods of time. A prepper might take note of the "best by" and "use by" dates and keep a keen eye out for dates that stretch out for lengthy periods. It's also helpful to recognize the difference between the terms.

Many folks don't take chances and they make sure to get through their food before the stamped-on deadline regardless of how it's presented. The dates, in either category, aren't required by government. "Use by" or "sell by" designations generally refer to the potential for spoilage. They're estimates and don't provide any set-in-stone guarantees. The "best by" designation, meanwhile, is indicative of flavor, texture or other factors that wouldn't bear on product safety.

Canned items produced by Hormel Foods, for instance, boast an indefinite shelf life. As surreal as it sounds, those foods would be safe for consumption long after we're gone. One could buy a can of SPAM today and fry it up in 40 years. The company's offerings, which include SPAM, its chili, corned beef hash and beef stew, carry "best by" dates on the packages. The company, however, indicates those dates might apply to flavor but have no

bearing on food safety as long as the seal remains intact and uncompromised.

A little bit of research might reveal a number of canned options that would do well in storage, particularly if it's a commonly used good that could go into a rotation. Del Monte Foods, for instance, indicates its canned goods have a shelf life, as it pertains to quality, of two

to three years. It's a good amount of time on its own. Though the foods would be best by the dates printed on the cans, they remain safe for consumption beyond that time so long as the container isn't dented or damaged, the company says.

Dried and freeze-dried foods offer years and sometimes decades of storage life. Powdered milk and eggs would provide for long storage life and also the nutrition and comfort of having those staple foods at hand regardless of whether they're available in fresh form. Dried beans will last forever as long as they're properly stored. They'd provide families with another source of protein to draw from.

Dried grains would provide for your carbo-

MRE meals come with all the fixings, and even some toilet paper.

Gardening is a common sense use of your land that provides a great deal to any household. It's a great hobby that gets you outdoors. It's enjoyable to very literally watch your efforts take root and grow into something valuable. Come harvest, there's something richly satisfying about meals that are made of your own time and work. You shouldn't discount another important quality of homegrown food: the prepper knows exactly where it came from and precisely what went into its creation.

Knowing what makes up your food takes on just a bit more nuance in today's era. Preppers who understand that gardening could move from a hobby to a necessity might think deeper and consider the very seeds they're putting into the ground. Those who are planting for richer flavors and those worried about long-term needs would ultimately come to the same conclusion. It makes the best sense to rely on heirloom varieties.

We've come to an era in which a few big corporations did some interesting work, came up with some interesting products and, as result, hold patents on many of the seeds available in those small packets down at the hardware store. They're engineered in a way that would benefit the simple gardener. They're also engineered in a way that would benefit the company's ultimate goals.

Those who plant for richer flavors and those worried about their long-term needs will want to use heirloom seeds.

The hybrid products on the market promote ease, better yield and resistance to disease. It's appealing to many for obvious reasons. The companies selling them fail to promote that there is limited to no ability to collect seeds from those plants that would allow gardeners to grow anew in the next season without another trip to the hardware store for yet another packet.

A wise prepper would recognize the value of having enough seeds to go one year in advance of the growing period to come. Collecting seeds and allowing a garden to rebuild itself from year to year is the ultimate exercise in self-reliance. Hybrid seeds are typically a one-year-and-done option. Those who gather seeds from non-heirloom plants and sow them in spring are bound to be disappointed by the next yield.

The real differences between heirloom and hybrid varieties go beyond planting. Those who are old enough and carry a good memory would recognize that produce today doesn't taste quite the same as that from the gardens of our grandparents. Taste is important. The seed companies aimed for a gardener's simplicity and their own bottom line. They were bound to lose something in the process.

Many like it easy, but easy rarely means better. It's worth looking around at seed options before planting. It's worth spending the additional time and care on plants that might not be as disease resistant as the modern hybrids. We get what we give. It could mean a tastier garden this year. It could mean reliable seeds for the next.

Preppers would recognize that immediate ease often tends to come at a price later down the road.

Planting and growing your own food is very rewarding.

115

hydrates and also store wonderfully. Rice will be just as good 20 years from now as it is today so long as it's properly kept. Quinoa, though pricey, might make for a good addition to the food locker. It's a dried, grain-like South American plant that'll carry a good, long shelf life. It's noted for high nutritional value that includes pretty high protein content for a plant-based food.

A number of foods people often go to for everyday nutrition and comfort could have some long-term potential. Wax-coated hard cheeses are known to last for significant periods without the need for refrigeration. Canned and pouched tuna and other seafoods typically have a shelf life of several years. Manufacturers generally recommend use within a year or two for taste, but again, the family that packs tuna salad sandwiches in the family's lunches on a fairly regular basis will be able to keep the stock on the fresh side by rotating.

Families might not go to a website and order a full year of shelf-stable food contingencies. They might, however, rely on some of those products as part of a more varied food plan. Starting at about $100, a prepper could buy a 5-gallon pail filled with a variety of individually packaged, freeze-dried vegetable servings.

A few cases of MREs might make up a significant portion of your meal planning if you're looking for ease and are only stretching out the plan for a few weeks of self-reliance. Those developing longer plans might still purchase a few cases to extend variety and flexibility. They're pre-packaged complete meals and come as varied as the selections in the grocery store's TV dinner case.

This was an MRE meal that the author shared with his wife — chicken pesto pasta, mixed fruit, bread with cheese bacon spread and vanilla pudding. You do not need to be in the field to enjoy an MRE.

They'll last on a shelf for five or more years if kept cool and dry.

Technology is lengthening the shelf lives of more foods all the time. Consumers are more regularly able to purchase irradiated food products. It's a process that utilizes radiation to kill of the bacteria that would contribute to food spoilage. Advances in aseptic processing are contributing to more shelf-stable food products. It's a process that's based in part around the use of sterile packaging.

In recent years, dairy companies have introduced shelf-stable milk that can sit unrefrigerated on a shelf for six months without going bad. The products rely on aseptic packaging after pasteurizing milk at higher than typical temperatures to assure that bacteria are killed off. A six-month shelf life isn't optimal for long-term food planning, but it's an interesting example of where technology is heading. It wasn't so long ago when people would've thought it a joke to have milk that doesn't require refrigeration.

Shelf-stable milk might be an option beyond powdered milk for the family that's planning for just a few months of contingency and depends upon their typical glasses of milk with breakfast and dinner. The families that find having regular, ready to drink milk important to their lives might switch to shelf-stable products, have a few months of supply at hand and keep the products stored away for emergency use in a rotation so it's used before expiration.

Having sufficient supplies of long stable foods is vital, though it's also important to assure it is stored properly. Preppers should have a cool and dry place to serve as the storage locker as a means of prolonging shelf life. The family with no other suitable options might put up some shelves in a spare bedroom.

Proper storage also means keeping food in a manner that wouldn't attract rodents that are always looking for that next big meal. No matter how well the home is sealed, it's no match for hungry mice that get a sense that food awaits. Five-gallon pails with sturdy lids — snap or screw-on — serve well for storing grains and other loose dried goods.

You should think through all the little details that could provide challenges should the time come to put your food planning to emergency use. For instance, you wouldn't have much luck with an electric can opener if the power is out. It makes sense to keep a manual model in your drawer full of kitchen gadgets.

You might consider methods to warm food if the power is out. It might mean a camp stove.

You might keep a good supply of propane or charcoal at the ready for the backyard grill. Some of the MREs on the market are self-heating.

Remember that while preparing for a disaster is about survival, it's also about comfort. Devise food plans that'll contribute to your family's wellbeing from both standpoints. Those who don't enjoy Spam shouldn't pack it away regardless of its endless shelf life. Build a food plan that matches with how your family would eat when it isn't dealing with all of those added stresses and emotions of emergency.

Those who begin to understand preparedness as a lifestyle will come to recognize readiness means more than packing away supplies. The notion of living a self-reliant lifestyle during the average day applies well to food and diet. Families might gain from a diet that goes beyond the offerings at the nearby supermarket.

Many would be able to take their emergency food plans beyond shelf-stable goods. Those who live in rural areas might approach their neighbors to talk about planning and get a sense of what they might be able to accomplish together if needs ever required. Those outside of the cities would very likely be able to maintain a strong sense of normalcy through teamwork if a disaster were to impact food supplies.

Those in rural areas would often have the capability to establish an economy on the smallest of scales. Bartering techniques might put everyone in better position. One neighbor might have some chickens and eggs while another raises beef or goats. One might have fruit trees while another is growing a large garden with 15 or more different vegetables. Some might have canned goods. Hunters and fishermen would have some commodities to offer. You would want to develop those relationships and have those conversations well before push comes to shove.

Those in urban and suburban areas, and even those with small properties, shouldn't

A propane stove, like this old Griswold model, cooks just like a house gas range in a pinch.

Mountain House, Wise foods and Backpackers Pantry are three big-name food companies that preppers should know. The nutritional values in their products will be similar to MREs, and they are more readily available.

discount gardening as a potential food source. Even those on properties with space for only a small garden tucked along the back fence might be surprised by how much food they'd be able to produce through spring and summer. Gardening requires some time investment each day, but it's as economical as it gets from the place of dollars and cents. It gives you a stronger appreciation of food, which can't be discounted in today's era.

There's nothing better than fresh vegetables from the garden. Even a few tomato plants, for instance, might yield more fruit than a family could reasonably eat. You could stew some and make soups and sauces to can for later use.

With a garden, you can make long-term, shelf stable foods of your own. Food dehydrators are fairly inexpensive and tremendous tools. With a few hours, you can take the garden-fresh vegetable that would normally decay in a week and turn it into a food that would be just as viable 10 years down the road.

Some are comfortable in giving a 30-year shelf life to some foods that have had their moisture removed. Those looking to prep inexpensively could find a dehydrator for $50 or less. You could vacuum seal dehydrated foods for an even better likelihood of long-term viability.

There's no way around it. Food planning will take some spending at the front end. Though when considering the importance of food to comfort and survival, it's an investment that can't be overlooked or under planned. When considered over the long term, planning provides preppers with a certain degree of economy. Even beyond gardening and hunting, preppers might well be able to eat cheaper.

Those who utilize chest freezers return to mind and offer an example of how storage and planning provides benefits that go even beyond readiness. Many have those freezers to provide the ability to buy meats in larger quantities after they go on a deep sale. They can freeze them and have plenty to eat over extended periods at lower costs. You could extend that to shelf-stable goods and build up on stock whether through in-store deals, coupons or bulk stores.

Shifting your mindset on food to the long term might well contribute to health. People are creatures of habit, and food marks an area where many could benefit from developing good ones. Modern society's relationship with food has, by many measures, fallen into a pretty unhealthy territory as a result of our convenience culture. The bad stuff is everywhere. Nourishing, balanced meals are too often supplanted by those quick and easy foods that come packed with fat, sodium, bad carbs and any number of unnatural ingredients carrying names most couldn't pronounce.

Too many are willing to sacrifice the healthy and wholesome for the easier items, particularly if it tastes good. It goes further to explain why appropriate planning is such a foreign concept to so many. Those who rely so heavily on unhealthy foods are demonstrating their lack of concern for what might sit around the next corner.

Efforts spent on preparing, whether for food or otherwise, mean doing better for your family. Our meals are important components of our lives, and with a little effort, preparing could mean better eating now and months ahead. Those approaching preparedness with the idea of having more comfort and confidence amid all of our world's uncertainties can't overlook the importance of food. It's tough to imagine much more taxing on our bodies or spirits than lacking variety, quality or simply enough on the daily dinner plate.

Boiling water or even cooking is not difficult on a white gas Coleman camp stove. They get hot.

ARE THEY WORTH THE TROUBLE?

It seems the jury is still out when it comes to the value of vitamin supplements. Reading three different articles about vitamins and other nutritional products on the market will likely provide three different expert opinions on their value or lack thereof in terms of improving your health. Some swear by them. Others don't bother.

Those who aren't convinced in their value have some valid arguments. If people eat proper diets that provide them with all the vitamins and minerals needed, it's safe to say they can get by without the hassle and additional expense. Certainly, generation after generation got by before those little, white bottles with childproof caps started showing up on the store shelves.

With that said, I take a multivitamin and other supplements tailored to some specific health considerations. Though a proper diet would indeed be sufficient to meet my needs, I consider a multivitamin an insurance policy should I leave a few blanks to fill in on any given day. Beyond the multivitamin, I take niacin based on the reports of its success for some in building good cholesterol while lowering the bad. I take a selenium supplement

knowing the soil in my region largely lacks that beneficial element.

In terms of preparation for a disaster recovery, multivitamins might well provide the right insurance policy should you lose the ability to provide the typical variety and balance available with a normal and typical diet. On the average day, vitamins would never be construed as a replacement for a proper diet. They're called supplements for a reason. A healthy day-to-day diet needs to be the first step.

Those who follow the directions on the bottles aren't going to experience harm by the common, well-established products on the market. Again, there are all sorts of debates on how much those products will benefit someone. A good prepper might want to read both sides of the debate on any given supplement before heading out to make the purchase.

If nothing else, there is something to be said for the placebo effect. Those who believe they're helping their bodies might actually do so regardless of the contents of that tablet. Your body might well respond to the mind's view of nutrition offered by the vitamins taken.

Every prepper will find his own best answers, whether it's vitamins or any other part of the plan. The experts might not agree on how much or whether a multivitamin will help. I tend to think it can't hurt.

Vitamins and supplements aren't for everyone, but the author believes they're a good insurance policy.

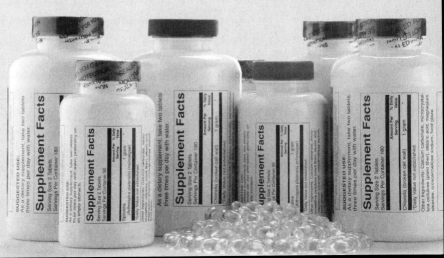

5

WATER

Drinking water is one of the things
we often take for granted, but it's
vital to have a reliable supply in a
disaster situation.

There isn't much in the world that's more important than water, or as easily forgettable. It's there at the turn of the faucet. It's ready and usually reliable.

Drinking water doesn't typically give rise to much thought. It's the simplest substance on the planet. You wouldn't pause to appreciate

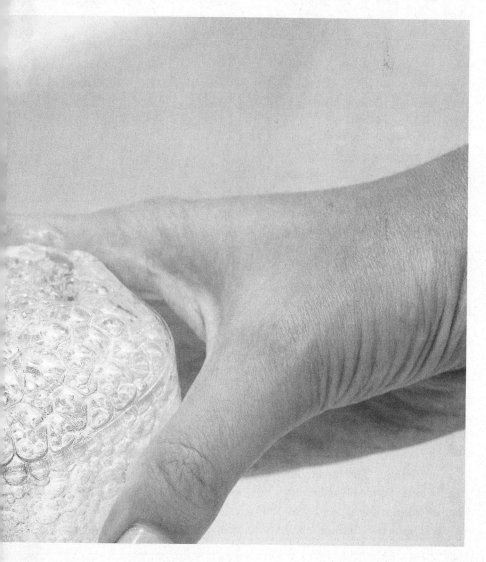

The author, far right, deals with a contaminated well at an Afghan local police outpost.

water safety or consider how you're promoting your wellbeing when waking thirsty and climbing out of bed for a quick drink. In essence, it's your body recognizing what doesn't always reach the intellect. There isn't much more imperative than water when it comes to maintaining your health.

Those new to prepping might have never figured that something of such little complexity could actually require a good degree of problem solving. The more complicated nature of water becomes clearer when recognizing its role to survival and then figuring out how the family would make it through should the typical methods of securing safe supplies run dry. Time is always of the essence when water isn't there.

Accounting for drinkable water is among the fundamental components of preparedness. It requires some earnest effort from those planning for a disaster aftermath. Safe water could become a matter of life or death for the unprepared. It's a basic necessity to living, and therefore, it's a top priority.

The rule of threes says it most clearly. Beyond lacking ability to maintain proper body temperature, a lack of fluids would most quickly lead to your death. The rule offers just three days without water before a person would succumb. It doesn't get much more pressing than that.

Unfortunately, water isn't a care-free contingency. It's heavy. It's bulky. If it isn't purified in some manner, the potential for contaminants would present a risk of illness that would make life far more difficult. It's an area of prepping that presents some challenges. Filling up a few big jugs and moving along to the next area of planning isn't getting the job done.

A lack of clean water and the inability to purify would become a huge concern for those who fall into survival situations or are otherwise away from the safety and security of the preps established at home. Physical difficulties would mount well in advance of three days should you fail to find a safe source for drinking. Preppers planning their stay-in-place strategies would want to think through all the possibilities that could impact water availability and devise several solutions that could account for family needs.

Planning for water sounds reasonable enough when it's broken down to the very basics. A good plan would include some amount of storage, an ability to collect water as well as having methods to make potentially dangerous water safe for drinking should situations require. Like most other areas of life, the devil lies in the details.

Water plans would look different depending on where you live. Those living on several acres out in the country would have the ability to store significant amounts of potable water. It wouldn't present too much concern. The family making its home in the small, urban, two-bedroom apartment might not be able to take their plans as far as they'd like from a storage aspect.

The means of collecting water from the environment would require far more work for those living in the deserts of the southwestern United States. Those living in the forested lands in the northeastern region of the country get plenty of rainfall and with the right containers, could store enough away. It goes to show the importance of preparation. Through planning, anyone — regardless of home — could come to some good solutions that would provide for appropriate safety.

Meeting the water component of a solid preparation plan requires a level of thought most fail to exercise. Clean and safe water is rarely an issue for families in this part of the world, and as such, it's not so seriously viewed as holding the potential for danger. Drinking water in the United States is generally regarded among the cleanest in the world.

Americans really are in a great spot. People often take appropriate caution regarding water safety when traveling abroad. Those same folks would crank the knob on a drinking fountain anywhere domestically without any degree of worry. Americans are fortunate on the average day to have such an important resource so readily available without any cause for second guessing. Prepping, though, isn't about the clear and bright, every day Saturday afternoon.

A variety of disaster situations could impede on your access to clean and drinkable water. Power outages could impact the abilities of homes to draw from their wells. Lengthy, widespread outages could mean some big troubles for the unprepared. Store shelves would empty of bottled products faster than you might imagine in such a circumstance.

Earthquakes could damage municipal mains. Tornadoes could just as easily damage piping or destroy filtration plants. The nation's water systems were listed as a key security priority after the Sept. 11 attacks in recognizing the widespread and deadly impact terrorists could have by contaminating supplies.

Water planning presents a wide variety of "what if?" possibilities to think about regardless of where you call home.

Flooding is commonplace, and among all natural disasters, it most often contaminates sources of drinking water. Flooding often causes more property damage in a given year in the United States than any other form of disaster. Floods also carry the real possibility of putting the public's heath at risk. They're tremendously difficult situations for families regardless of

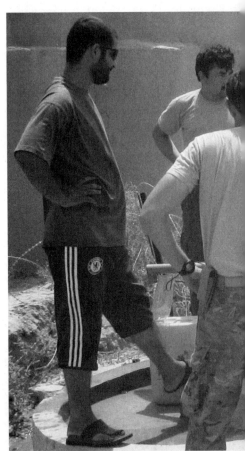

their scale.

Water systems are among the biggest concerns for government units in regard to flooding, both as waters begin to rise and onward through the recovery phase. When floods occur, encroaching waters usher bacteria, chemicals, sewage, oil and a host of other contaminants picked up along the way into private wells and in through public systems. Families couldn't always count on a speedy return to normalcy.

Those who draw from wells would likely require some testing for contamination after floodwaters recede. Wells could potentially need some remediation before homeowners are given the go-ahead to resume life as normal. Those provided for through municipal systems are often subject to boil orders after floods. What's very simple in the day-to-day could become a major inconvenience or worse after

There isn't much more imperative than water when it comes to maintaining your health. It should be a key aspect of any survival plan.

a disaster. Proper planning provides the best chances to safely and comfortably bridge the gap.

The body's water requirements might contribute to the challenge of meeting emergency needs in some cases. Few people consider how much fluid we consume on a daily basis or how often we drink. Consumption needs might not seem like much as you go about your daily activities. Water storage and collection, however, could get tricky for some in recognizing the significant amount of space it would take to house the volumes of fluids we require for everyday health when compounded over longer periods of time.

Experts say the typical person needs two to three liters of fluids on a daily basis just to make up for what the body loses as a matter of living. People lose fluids in a number of ways from sweating to breathing. Those average requirements don't account for the water you would need to wash up or prepare meals if typical supplies weren't there. Those engaged in the hard work that typifies survival or recovery situations would sweat far more than normal and thus need yet more fluid intake to maintain proper balance.

It's interesting to think about how preppers would manage if their plans were limited to storage alone. Water requirements

would add up quickly. A common recommendation suggests storing a minimum of one gallon of water per person, per day to account for consumption, cooking and sanitation. Consider the math for a family of four.

The family that tucked away 12 gallons is covered for three days. At three weeks, they'd need 84 gallons to get by. A prepper who hasn't looked beyond collection and is hoping to cover that same family for three months would need to have 360 gallons of water available. It's an amount that translates to just more than 48 cubic feet of space.

The dedicated, take-no-chances prepper who's relying on storage and living in an urban or suburban environment might have some dismay. He'd probably come to realize there's no easy way to put up a full-year supply of water for the entire family in the same fashion he's planned for food. A 1,500-gallon water tank would provide appropriate space for that year-long supply. That option, however, isn't one likely to go over well with either the neighbors or the zoning department. Above-ground models in that capacity come in at a diameter of near eight feet and stand about five feet tall. Water takes up some serious real estate.

The amounts required for health and the space needed to keep it aren't mentioned to overwhelm but

simply to suggest a good water plan is best achieved through a number of strategies. Thoughts might start with an assessment of how much you could reasonably store for a stay-at-home recovery. You might collect rainwater as a means to extend your contingencies. A prepper would then consider other options such as

A high-quality water filter, like this one from Big Berkey, is a simple way to have clean water no matter what.

129

filtering and methods of chemical disinfection that would allow you to render water safe whenever needed and wherever you might be.

Ensuring safe and sufficient water takes some know-how and the right gear. A vigilant prepper would always have some means at quick reach to assure sufficient, safe fluids in the event you're left without. Planning would extend beyond the home to the car. It's smart to have a well-built go-bag, and water is an important component. It wouldn't necessarily take the disaster that's affecting thousands or millions of people for you to have to worry about where you'd get your next drink.

You could imagine any number of hypothetical situations that could put you at danger as it pertains to water needs. The hunter who drove deep into the forest with nothing more than a few snacks, a gun, ammo and his canteen could stumble into crisis if the truck battery went dead and he was beyond the reach of cell phone reception. The avid, though unprepared boater stuck out on the ocean would encounter some bitter irony in being surrounded by water on all sides yet being unable to take a drink.

Giving due thought to water and unraveling the potential emergencies that would impact supplies is the first big stride forward. Different authorities offer different sug-

gestions for household planning. FEMA suggests a minimum three-day, stored water supply for each member of the household. Some groups, including the American Red Cross, go further in suggesting at least two weeks of water storage for emergency use.

Preppers would want to do better. Both three-day and two-week suggestions offer goals that are achievable, provide some level of cushion and wouldn't overwhelm families when recognizing that most people fail to think even that far ahead. Common sense, however, wouldn't allow for too much comfort

in a plan limited to a short-term supply with nothing else to provide some appropriate back-up.

Our continual need for fluids is really what pushes the issue. You could go for several days without food if the situation demanded. It would be a mighty uncomfortable time, but you would probably be no worse for the wear when finally coming by that next meal. Your survival mindset would allow you to push through the misery and accomplish the other efforts necessary toward

Store-bought containers offer the most convenient way to build your water storage.

your safety and wellbeing. The rule of threes sets death at three weeks for those with nothing to eat.

No one can do without water even for short stretches without experiencing some real impacts on health. Fluid loss on the body could quickly leave you incapacitated and utterly unable to move forward. Limiting a plan to a short-term supply is better than having no plan at all. Certainly, emergency situations of three days or less are common enough and more likely to impact households than the major disaster. A stash of 12 to 14 gallons for the family of four would suffice in those scenarios.

However, you should question how much you're willing to gamble with your family's safety. The clock on your wellbeing starts ticking as soon as the water supply runs dry. Someone working hard under hot conditions without access to fluids could start to feel the early effects of dehydration in as quickly as an hour or two. There's a reason why sporting events have all of those Gatorade jugs sitting along the sidelines for athletes to draw from.

Needs truly are immediate. The three days offered by the rule of threes tends to suggest a bit more leeway than you would truly have when dehydration issues settle in. Death at three days is only part of the story when thinking about the urgency of water requirements.

The rule glosses over the serious tolls that lacking fluids have on the body all along the way.

Living is a relative term. Certainly, you might very well be able to draw a breath while lying incoherent as the three-day mark approaches without fluid intake. A person even after one day of lacking fluids could struggle mightily. Weakness and that very general "unwell" feeling could become a big roadblock to safety at the very earliest stages of dehydration. As a lack of fluids persists, you would move further down the slope and lack the physical ability to tackle all of the other challenges that come in a survival situation or disaster aftermath soon enough.

Health officials suggest those who are experiencing symptoms of dehydration quit their activity and get some adequate rest. A survival situation might render that option impossible. Critical dangers would surface well before the end-of-the-line benchmark.

Everyday experience speaks loudly. Most people wouldn't need the rule to have a decent grasp of the body's reliance on fluids. Heading out for a jog or even mowing the lawn beneath the bright sun on a sweltering summer day often provides reminder enough of the body's dependence. The body responds and tends to offer some quick reminders when hydration falls beneath an optimal level. There isn't much less comfortable than a dry and deep thirst.

The impacts on the body run far deeper. Dehydration at even its earliest stages is unpleasant. You might get a pretty debilitating headache.

Water loss lends to a drop in blood pressure and a rapid heart rate. Your body temperature would begin to climb without the fluids necessary to produce adequate sweat. Those suffering from dehydration often experience dizziness in the early onset.

You could fall into a coma as dehydration reaches its critical stages. Severe cases, if not fatal, could result in kidney failure and permanent brain damage. What's most scary is that all of those symptoms could come to bear in such a short period of time.

That's where preparedness comes to play. The only solution to avoid those dangers is to drink enough. For preppers, it means having adequate access to what the body needs and no less.

Therein lie s another difficulty presented by water. It isn't contained well within any set-in-stone, black-and-white rules. "Enough" isn't so easily defined. Estimates for fluid intake speak to the average person on the average day. Every person and each situation is different. Disaster or survival, meanwhile, is far from what you could ever call average.

The environment and workload could quickly require you to ramp up your fluid intake. The person who is losing water to sweat while chopping up wood on a humid summer afternoon would obviously need more than the person sitting in an air conditioned house. Those chopping wood side by side on that same afternoon might have different needs. Differing physical abilities might play a role, and frankly, some folks have more active sweat glands than others.

Maintaining proper health requires paying closer attention to what the body says than to what any guidelines suggest. You could have that full three liters and still encounter some dehydration issues. When working in disaster zones, it was typical to see charts reminding people to keep watch on the color of their urine as a reliable guide to their levels of hydration.

A properly hydrated person would have clear urine. Cloudier urine means you should be drinking more. The level of your water needs and the dangers presented by dehydration grow higher as the color grows darker. You should consider the frequency of urination in addition to the color. It could be a highly dangerous sign of advancing dehydration if you aren't expelling urine with typical regularity.

The unpredictability of your water needs underscores the importance of having more than stored supplies as insurance should water safety become an issue. The daily gallon per person would likely suffice for those living in a cooler, Northern climate. It could prove woefully inadequate for those living amid a hot and humid Louisiana summer. No one can really know with any kind of accuracy what the family would need. Your health could suffer greatly if you decided to resign yourself to daily rations determined by the remaining quantities of water on hand.

Right tools, right know-how

Take a moment to consider the helplessness you might feel when suffering from thirst and having no way to alleviate it. When it comes down to it, there are few to no good options left for the unprepared at the point of a water emergency. It would take some degree of luck to pull through.

Certainly, natural water sources are plentiful in much of the country. Drinking untreated water without knowledge of its safety simply couldn't be regarded as the lesser of two evils when stacked against the urgency presented by dehydration. It would really only serve to make a bad situation far worse.

The imagery of the frontiersman dipping his hands into the cold, rushing stream to alleviate his thirst is history that wouldn't be all that smart to mimic in the modern day and age. Natural waterways might look clear and pristine, yet could be teeming with a variety of nasty elements whether from agricultural runoff or chemical toxins ushered in from an industrial setting. You could never know. Many people each year become ill from inadvertent swallowing while swimming in public waters like lakes, oceans and sometimes even chlorinated pools.

The Giardia lamblia parasite is one that's all too common in natural waters, whether it's a stagnant pond or even the clear, trickling stream. It could become an issue in wells and municipal systems after disaster. The parasite presents a host of issues from stomach cramping and bloating to severe diarrhea. Cryptosporidium is another microorganism common to water and could also leave you with diarrhea, stomach pain, nausea and vomiting.

Those in survival mode would be wise to stop and think of those illnesses should natural waters give rise to any temptation. Consuming contaminated water regardless of your extreme thirst could exacerbate your already high risks in a water emergency. Diarrhea and vomiting would significantly speed the dehydration of your body. De-

hydration happens quickly without the added push of a parasitic illness.

In understanding water's urgency, those prepping wouldn't leave anything to chance, whether at home or elsewhere. Preppers who are beyond their homes should have their go-bags within reach and packed with gear to account for food, water and shelter. The water component of the bag would include some clean water to get through the day and ways to collect water and render it safe.

The survival situation best illustrates the importance of being able to provide for water in manners beyond the stored supply. One gallon of water weighs in at more than eight pounds. The go-bag, which is designed for three days, wouldn't serve a survivalist well if it includes 24 pounds of water weight. The space needed to store it would alone make it unreasonable.

For a point of comparison, you could purchase a lightweight tent for your go-bag that can sleep two people that comes in at less than four pounds. Meanwhile, the one-gallon jug at twice its weight would fall short of providing proper hydration for those same two people over that first day. There are better solutions. It starts with some understanding.

You might keep in mind that rainwater is safe for consumption

so long as it's collected in a manner in which it isn't exposed to contaminants. Rain water is a great option from the standpoint of home storage. It's free. It's self-replenishing. In a survival situation, it certainly isn't reliable unless, of course, your hardships correspond with some storms pushing through.

Some natural waters offer those in need with safer bets than others. Springs and artesian wells have traditionally held as safe for drinking. You might nonetheless take some degree of caution in recognizing surrounding ground contamination could impact safety. Those collecting from natural waters with the intent of purifying should look to draw from flowing sources, rather than stagnant, if it's at all possible.

A pot and a heat source might be the simplest reliable way to make sure your water is safe to drink. Boiling would kill the host of micro-organisms that present the biggest risks of waterborne illness. It's generally agreed that keeping water at a rolling boil for five minutes would eliminate the risks posed by bacteria and parasites. Those living in higher altitudes would want to extend that time a bit. It's ready for consumption after it cools.

If you have room, large containers like these 55-gallon food-grade drums could be a good solution for water storage.

Some would argue that a lesser time than five minutes would make water safe enough for drinking. There are experts who would say that one minute sufficiently does the job. A disaster aftermath or survival situation isn't the proper time to take unnecessary risks that could make an already difficult situation potentially dire though. On the opposite end, you might remember that boiling for a time longer than necessary would only turn more of that water supply into escaping steam. Five minutes, it seems, provides a pretty good compromise.

There are a few chemical means available that would increase your chances of safety when situations require drinking from questionable sources. You might pack away some iodine tablets in the go-bag or have a supply stashed in the car. They are specifically manufactured for water purification and are typically available at camping and sporting goods shops. It's a small, light-weight and inexpensive back-up option, but it's also one that carries some cause for uneasiness.

Iodine tablets are an effective means of killing many dangerous bacteria, including E. Coli, though iodine might still leave you at risk of cryptosporidium infection. It isn't the most convenient or pleasant means of achieving safe water. The method typically takes a half hour or longer, and the iodine leaves a pretty strong taste behind.

Typical household bleach pro-vides another way to disinfect. Like iodine pills, bleach fails to provide a foolproof means of safety. It does improve your chances of avoiding illness. Chlorine bleach kills some

With proper preparation, most water sources can be used to sustain life.

but not all of the microorganisms that could present health hazards.

The U.S. Environmental Protection Agency recommends boiling over bleach if it's an available option. Those relying on bleach would put eight drops into a gallon of water to disinfect. If you are relying on that method, you should stir well and leave the water to sit for a half hour before consumption.

The cheap, run-of-the-mill bleach is the best stuff when it comes to water safety. Be mindful to use regular, unscented bleach. It usually comes at a 5- to 5.25-percent chlorine concentration. Color-safe and pleasant-smelling products, as you could imagine, are better suited for your laundry duties than they are for your drinking supplies.

The best tools for assuring water safety take a bit of an investment. Filtering systems — both for the home and the go-bag — would nonetheless go a long way to offer you some peace of mind as to the viability of your water plans. The best filters could turn the murkiest of water into something clear, safe and ultimately drinkable from the standpoint of flavor.

You would want to make sure to spend appropriately for high-quality products in recognizing it's a matter of family safety. You should read before buying to assure the considered product is reliable and capable of removing microorganisms among other contaminants. Many of the lesser priced and readily available filtering units found at most stores were designed from the perspective of improving the flavor of water rather than addressing contamination.

As for home systems, Berkey filters are pretty highly regarded among preppers and the survivalist community. They've been shown to reduce a variety of contaminants to undetectable levels, whether its viruses, bacteria, parasites or nasty chemicals that could become an issue during a disaster. They are, however, pricey. The smallest models run more than $200. Bigger units would make far more sense when purchased with preparedness in mind, and particularly if purchased for a household of several people.

Those preparing their go-bags should consider a hand-pump purification system. The small, lightweight pumps, available from companies including MSR and Katadyn, very reliably remove contamination from natural water sources. They make for clear and clean water that you could pump into a bucket or perhaps a camel-back backpack. The pumps start at less than $100 and range up to $300 or more for some models. It's money well spent for those who spend time in the outdoors, and they could prove priceless should you end up in survival mode.

Many of the highly rated filters, whether designed for the home or go-bag, are known to do some pretty amazing work even with some pretty disgusting water. It's nonetheless in the best interest of users to use the cleanest water available. At the very least, those resigned to using debris-laden water might want to run it through cheese cloth to remove larger bits of sediment. You could also run water through a parfait of sand and gravel that would recreate ground filtering and accomplish the same. Filters become dirtier more quickly without that bit of forethought.

Those in water emergencies might use some of these methods together to better assure safety. Boiling, for instance, would kill off all those nasty little bugs, but it would leave a rough situation for the taste sensitive. Brown and foul smelling water could be difficult for many people to stomach. Boiling would offer some guarantees as far as pathogens go. A filter would remove all of the other impurities, leaving clear water that people are used to drinking. The same would hold true in removing iodine and chlorine flavors left behind by tablets and bleach, respectively.

All of those solutions offer varying degrees of safety but also come with the assumption that water — whether safe or not — is readily available. Those living in regions where water isn't so plentiful should have the goods needed to create solar stills stowed away in their cars and go-bags. It doesn't take very much and could become a life saver.

Solar stills are simple tools that rely on sunlight and condensation to draw clean, pure water from the ground or available vegetation. Dry

riverbeds provide great locations for set-up so long as those in survival mode are able to find them. The first step in that case would require digging down far enough to find some moisture.

The still itself is a cup or some other form of collection basin and a sheet of plastic. It really is that simple. You would put the cup into the hole and secure the plastic over the top, whether by rocks or whatever is available to hold it in place.

From there, you would put a small rock at the center of the plastic and above the cup in order to create a conical

MSR makes great water filtration units, The author likes this model because it fits on large-mouth water bottles and bladders.

shape. Sunlight does the remainder of the work. Pure water evaporates from the sun's heat, leaving impurities behind. Those drops of pure, contaminant-free water cling to the plastic and dribble down into the cup. Some people run a straw down beneath the plastic and into their collection basin so they can drink off the water as it collects.

Those unable to find dry riverbeds could fill the hole with whatever vegetation they can find and draw out the moisture from those plants in the same fashion. Any moisture would suffice. You could urinate in the hole before putting down the cup and separate that bit of water from the remainder of its substance.

Time and quantities could present issues for those who have to rely on solar stills for collection. Those caught in areas without sufficient water would want to put priority on still set-up at the very early stages of an emergency. You might want to have a few smaller solar stills going or a large enough still to draw off water sufficient to keep up with the body's needs.

Contingencies can only work if you are vigilant enough to always have them at the ready.

A hand-pump purification system can reliably remove contamination from natural water sources.

It's typical for travelers to forget a thing or two from time to time, though the go-bag isn't the item to let slip from the mind. The rule of threes as it applies to water means just the same should you become lost or stranded as it would after the big disaster.

Those dedicated to readiness would be wise to keep some drinking water in their vehicles. It's crucial to have some ability to stay healthy should a crash, empty gas tank or engine troubles leave you in a place where you couldn't expect immediate aid. It isn't unreasonable to think you could find yourself beyond reach of safety for several days. Without water, several days might as well be an eternity.

You might consider your environment when extending plans and strategies to the day-to-day potential for danger. If you became stuck in the middle of nowhere in a Northern winter, you could make do from a water perspective by melting snow. Like rainwater, a fresh white blanket of snow isn't going to present danger of contamination.

At the far opposite end, a motorist traveling through hot, remote and arid lands out West could quickly find himself in a potentially deadly situation for no reason but the lack of water if the car went off the road and became stuck in a ra-vine. You might consider stashing a few gallons of water in the trunk to provide safety and a valuable bit of time should troubles come to pass. Preppers would keep the water pump or solar still materials at easy reach should any emergency stretch further than the contents of your water bottles.

Home planning is also at its best when residents have multiple options in place to make sure everyone is covered for water for however long it takes before safety returns. A disaster could make life more difficult for a pretty good stretch of time. Water dangers might not be the most frequent or frequently discussed of emergencies, though that's no good excuse to relax your efforts.

Government units certainly keep an eagle's eye on water quality. All of the best efforts, however, still fall short of providing rock-solid guarantees. Situations that compromise water safety happen from time to time in the United States. They occasionally happen absent the destructive forces of natural disaster and despite intensive monitoring and strict regulations.

Two widespread events of recent decades go to show water security isn't foolproof. America's largest historical outbreak of waterborne illness came out of Milwaukee, and we're not talking about the 1800s when science and capabilities were far from today's standards. In 1993, problems at one of its water filtration plants spread cryptosporidium through the city over the course of two weeks. The outbreak sickened more than 400,000 and led to the deaths of more than 100 of the city's most vulnerable residents.

In 2010, nearly 2 million people in and near Boston were under a boil order for three days after a major water pipe broke and brought concern of contamination. Stores sold out of bottled water quickly. Officials there went so far as to request that bottled water companies increase shipments. Authorities went to great lengths to make sure affected residents promptly knew of the potential danger.

Disaster is a more likely source of water dangers. Boil orders were commonplace in many areas along the Gulf Coast after hurricanes Katrina and Rita made landfall in 2005. Providing for safety took significant time in some areas. Officials in New Orleans were only able to lift the first order in a section of the city more than a month

after Katrina struck the coast. It took more than a year before the entire city had water safe enough to consume without putting it over the stove to kill off potential contaminants.

Preppers have options. Filters are important. Storage makes sense.

Those who have $2,000 or more burning a hole in their pockets can go to several online retailers special-izing in survival and readiness and buy full-year supplies of canned drinking water. The cans boast a 30-year shelf life. Like food, those packages account only for one person's needs. You certainly wouldn't need to spend that kind of money, particularly on a substance that regularly falls from the sky. At that price, many would instead opt for whiskey.

Water filtration pumps can clean up almost any water source, but it's best to use the cleanest water available.

Store-bought containers, whether single-serving bottles or gallon jugs, would offer the most convenient way to build your water storage. They're safe, sealed and ready to put away. Gallon jugs generally come quite cheaply, and you might build up your supply by putting a few extra in the cart during each of the weekly, forthcoming shopping trips.

Different experts have different opinions on shelf life. The U.S. Food and Drug Administration claims properly stored bottled water has an indefinite shelf life. The FDA notes water could take on an off-odor or taste if it sits too long.

Others suggest a shelf life of a year or two. You can find "use by" dates carried on some bottled waters. There's concern in some circles that chemicals from the containers could begin to leach into the water over time and present some health issues.

Those concerned about water quality and safety could split the difference by rotating their emergency supplies and using those bottles nearing "use by" dates for day-to-day consumption. If you haven't rotated and have a big supply beyond expiration dates, you could alleviate worries by running the water through a filter. Having several means of providing for safety takes away a lot of the stress that a water emergency stands to present.

Bottling from the tap is another option and one yet cheaper than provided by the grocery store. You could use empty two-liter soda bottles or previously used water bottles. You might buy a few of the five-gallon jugs that top water coolers whether or not there's a cooler to place it upon.

You should thoroughly clean whatever container you choose with hot water and dish soap. You could use some bleach and water for sanitizing. Make sure to rinse well before use. Adding a few drops of bleach to the filled containers would work well to prevent bacteria growth that wouldn't be an issue with sealed, store-bought products.

The U.S. Military's canteens and camelback hydration pack are great ways to store water.

Mother Nature freely offers a key piece of the preparation puzzle to every household on a fairly regular basis. Too many people with too little thought just allow that wonderful resource to soak into the soil. Collecting water takes a little work and a bit of spending. Then again, having a good amount in storage would offer any family far less cause for worry after a disaster.

Those who are connected to a municipal water supply are at someone else's mercy when it comes to a major survival need. It's a big-time need that takes some big-time thinking. Aside from those who live in multi-unit buildings, anyone would have the ability to store away at least some amount of water.

For some, it might not be a matter of storage. There are a lot of properties out there that once had wells and were since brought into a municipal supply. If the well is there, it doesn't hurt to hook it up. It's a ready supply of clean water just waiting for use.

Others would need to collect what they can. Rain barrels are available for $100 or less. Even the smallest properties would have some room to take advantage. It's no longer a matter of sticking an eyesore out into the yard. You could purchase barrels that hold 50 gallons or more that come shaped like rocks or urns that would blend nicely into the landscaping. Place one at each of the downspouts. Those who haven't had rain barrels might be surprised by the amounts they'd collect from that single inch of rain that rolls off the roof.

Those who want to take the next step could transfer water from the barrels to a storage bladder. It would open space for additional collection in the barrels at the next rainfall. A 1,000-gallon water bladder would tuck very nicely in the crawl space available under a number of homes.

You could run that water through a filter to pull away anything collected from the rooftop and have good, pure drinking water. A family could use it for cooking and sanitation. Water collection and storage, meanwhile, doesn't have to be limited to emergency needs. Mother Nature will refill what you decide to use. You could spend some of that water on the garden or the lawn. The water from the hose is money spent for those drawing off of a municipal system. Collecting from the clouds might save a few dollars.

Those who aren't collecting rainwater are really missing out. There's little in this world we're given for free. Further, it's a critical resource. It's truly worth taking the fullest advantage any household is able.

Whether hand-filled or store-bought, a family would want at least a couple weeks' worth of ready-to-drink, easy-to-access water at hand. Cool, darker places are best for storage. You should then think of ways to have water available beyond the bottles and jugs. Those who have hot tubs or swimming pools have a big supply of water at the ready for use in emergency. They could use it for sanitation or run it through the filter to provide for consumption needs.

Those who live in a rural setting could purchase a storage tank and rely on rain clouds to fill it up. It would easily solve your water needs for the long-term. Plastic tanks that can hold 1,000 gallons typically start at about $500. Bladders that provide high-quantity storage capabilities are also available. They offer a greater convenience in the fact that they can be folded up and easily moved if not in use.

Either option is best teamed with a decent filter. You could use such a large supply of water in a variety of means. Families could draw from the tank for showers. They could use it for cooking. If it's for drinking, the best bet is to filter it to make perfectly certain it's

clear and healthy regardless of how long it sat.

Bladders could very well provide a workable option for even those with very limited storage space. It's an interesting innovation. They come in a variety of sizes, from the very small all the way up to more than 200,000 gallons in capacity. Some homes might not be able to accommodate a 500-gallon bladder. Residents with very limited space might well find a good spot for 25, 50 or even 100 gallons.

Those on smaller properties

might not test the tempers of their neighbors with a yard-consuming tank. Still, a few rain barrels tucked away in the backyard make plenty of sense, are fairly commonplace and would push plans forward. It's additional clean, drinkable water at the ready. At 50 gallons apiece, two would mean three more weeks of insurance for the family of four. A good rain or two in that period would replace some of what was taken.

Preppers have plenty of options as it pertains to water. There's no perfect plan for everyone. Water, meanwhile, provides for one of the more interesting portions of the overall plan. There is nothing simpler, but water's place in our lives is anything but. It makes up 71 percent of Earth's surface, though dying from a lack of water is still a true and honest threat.

The rule of threes doesn't offer leeway, and therefore it's imperative to get a strong plan in place. Having the methods to achieve safe water wherever you might be is having the ability to avert catastrophe. It's worth considering when filling up the next glassful.

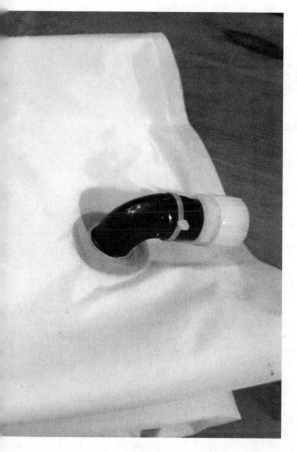

Small bladder tanks like this 15-gallon model are a good option for those with very limited storage space.

6

SHELTER

Bitter cold can be extremely
dangerous in a disaster situation.

Surviving and thriving amid times of strife requires a lot for people to think about. Those in the midst of an emergency would want to keep one very specific number at the top of mind. There isn't a figure more important to human life than 98.6 degrees. It's the normal, healthy temperature of the human body. Biology

doesn't allow for you to waver much on either side of that marker for long without running into some dire consequences.

High heat brings just as much, if not more, danger than bitter cold. The potential for trouble isn't limited to extreme temperatures. A variety of factors could play a role in moving body temperature off its balance. Alcohol, for instance, can lower your body temperature despite its tendency to make a person feel warm. Some medications elevate body temperature and could put you at risk should summer temperatures climb beyond bearable.

Anyone could very quickly fall into serious trouble, regardless of cause, by moving beyond or below 98.6 degrees by even just a few degrees. It's critical to have a way to correct. Life requires a pretty delicate balance.

The body's temperature presents the most crucial, basic factor of survival. It's a piece of preparedness that demands utmost attention, though it doesn't always get its due as a top-flight concern. Many of those who haven't thought about preparation would more quickly think to food or water as bigger matters if quizzed on life's key needs. Without proper shelter, you wouldn't get far enough along for those otherwise vital components to even come into play.

For a prepper, the ability to account for your body temperature provides the very meaning of shelter. Most tend to think of shelter as a place in which you could take refuge from the elements. That's an important part of the overall picture.

Preppers, though, go a step further and rely on the term to describe any method that would allow you to keep your body temperature as close to the safe and healthy norm as possible. Shelter could be a shade tree or a cold bottle of water for those starting to feel weary when caught outdoors in high humidity under a blazing sun. Shelter could be a parka, hat and gloves for those stuck in the midst of unbearably cold temperatures.

The little things sometimes make a big difference. The prepper would recognize shelter in something as simple as a silicone tarp. It might be the clothes on your back. Shelter could be the small box of waterproof matches in the front pocket should you need to get a fire going. The key point at any time, in any place or in any situation is to stick very closely to 98.6. Life depends on it.

Shelter for those struggling through a disaster's aftermath would most often fall within the everyday, dictionary definition. A family could often meet its needs from the home and better so with

the right contingencies in place. Those who live in areas prone to cold might recognize that the gas or electric furnace is a great tool, but they aren't foolproof. Preparing would take furnace loss into account. Those who live in areas prone to extreme heat might think about how they'd get through without the central air conditioner. Those who are lost or stranded have an entirely different set of issues to work through to maintain that essential balance.

The high level of danger presented by a lack of proper shelter should promptly draw a prepper's focused attention. If 98.6 degrees is the most important number to your wellbeing, a related figure that's provided for by the rule of threes follows very closely behind. Those pushed far enough from their normal body temperatures have only three hours to cool off or warm up depending on their predicaments.

Hyperthermia, when the body's temperature moves and sticks at more than 100 degrees, is a constant problem in places like Afghanistan.

It's a frightening number. Three hours is often a pretty tight deadline for even many of the inconsequential affairs in your day-to-day living. The rule of threes tells us that short period — the length of the typical, televised sporting event — is all that would separate life and death without a way to warm or cool your body. The clock begins to tick just as soon as the body temperature sufficiently moves off its norm. Those in survival mode have no time to spare.

The cold side of the equation is medically referred to as hypothermia. A person reaches that condition when the body's core temperature falls to 95 degrees or less. It's amazing to think how much just 3.6 degrees means to our wellbeing.

It's a dangerous enough state of affairs when looked upon by the rule of threes, but more so as it's a risk that could sneak up on those who haven't properly thought ahead. Those who don't know the warning signs could face tremendous risks as the symptoms begin to set in. The symptoms often come to bear gradually enough that someone suffering might not even recognize there's anything wrong.

Further, the very nature of the symptoms can add another layer of worry as hypothermia progresses. Its toll on the body has a certain way of masking the danger. Too few of those who live in cold climate areas, for example, tend to think all that much about shivering. It happens.

The people who live in the country's coldest spots are pretty hardy and many might view that bodily response to the elements as something to tough out whether they're at work or play. It should instead provide a big red flag when they've been out in the cold for an extended period. It's among the first notable signs of the body temperature's downward fall. Those who ignore that warning sign will soon enough lose it. The shivering would begin to decrease and eventually disappear as hypothermia grows worse.

Those suffering from hypothermia often begin to experience confusion and disorientation as the condition worsens. Many people could attest that they haven't made the best decisions in regard to their wellbeing while intoxicated. It really isn't all that different.

The point might eventually come during hypothermia at which you would lack the mental wherewithal to recognize or understand the severity of what's happening to your body. It could go well beyond your capacity to recognize you're only in need of some warmth. Those suffering would eventually lose consciousness should they lack the means of bringing up their body temperatures. At that point, you would be getting pretty close to death.

It's a condition that further illustrates why it's so vital to learn about and understand all of the big-time risks you could face in a survival situation or disaster aftermath. Hypothermia is most likely to occur in the bitterest of temperatures, though not necessarily so. Many would fail to consider the possibility of dying for a lack of warmth at arguably comfortable temperatures. It's all the same a threat amid tem-

This yellow tent folds up to the size of a soda can. It's a good option for a go-bag so you always have shelter available in case you have to avoid cold winds, rain or the hot sun.

peratures of 40 degrees or more.

Hyperthermia, conversely, becomes a concern when the body's temperature moves and sticks at more than 100 degrees. Many of those suffering the condition have dehydration issues in conjunction with their dangerously high body temperature. Severe cases

Wood stoves provide lots of heat, require no electricity and also give you a place to cook and heat water for bathing.

154

on the high side of temperature imbalance might also result in a state of confusion among those suffering. As the condition persists, blood pressure would drop. Organs would eventually fail. The person suffering from hyperthemia would lose consciousness and die pretty quickly from the lack of some means to slowly and steadily cool back down.

Those who know and respect the risks and symptoms have already made big strides. Those cold, shivering and noticing a bit of clumsiness, for instance, should know enough to make warmth their very lone priority. Those out and about among those brutally hot temperatures of mid to late summer who experience nausea, headaches and dizziness should recognize it's time to head into the air conditioning or any other cooler spot without delay.

Shelter is always job No. 1. People have certainly been blessed with intellect and ingenuity. As far as our world's walking and breathing beings go, humankind came up on the short end as far as an ability to manage physically amid the challenging elements brought forth by nature. People just aren't built for weather.

The prompt nature by which you could go from healthy to deceased by virtue of temperature alone should never move far from your mindset. It's particularly important for those who are out and beyond their everyday comforts. Shelter demands that people think ahead. Those who don't take proper precaution stand to run into potentially life-threatening scenarios well before loved ones might ever consider them as missing or endangered.

It might be the hiker or cyclist who ventured out too far from home without first taking a glance at that day's weather forecast. He might have left in a sweatshirt recognizing his exertion would make up for the chilly temperatures whether it's in early spring or late fall. If he's caught in a pounding rain — and even if temperatures are well above freezing — severe dangers would become imminent. He could very well die without finding some way to dry off and find warmth within three hours.

Someone beyond the reach of relief from the opposite side of the temperature scale could just as quickly run into a potentially fatal scenario. It could be the same hiker or biker who embarked on one of those burning hot, late summer days in the Midwest. It could be someone whose car ran out of gas 25 miles outside the nearest town on a dry, scalding day in the Southwest.

Your level of risk depends on the work done in advance. A prepper should always have means to manage from the perspective of temperature whether at home or while away. In some cases, it's a matter of knowledge. In other cases, it's having the right gear. A mere three hours moves by quickly, particularly so for those experiencing periods of high stress. It doesn't take much.

The risks are real. Exposure to high heat or extremely cold temperatures takes lives on an annual basis. The Centers for Disease Control and Prevention cited an average of 689 annual deaths in the United States attributed to exposure to excessive natural cold in the period from 1979 to 2002. The nation averaged an annual 569 heat-related deaths in the period from 1999 through 2005, according to the CDC.

It goes to show that disaster doesn't always have to mean the big, attention-grabbing weather events such as tornadoes, earthquakes or regional flooding. The extreme hot or cold weather events that strike many communities a few times every year might very well qualify as disasters on individual scales depending on the abilities of people to regulate their body temperatures.

Severe temperatures rarely result in big, national headlines. It isn't as dramatic as the destructive earthquake. The toll taken on our country by temper-

When electricity fails, an Aladdin lamp is a good option. They can provide enough heat to take the chill off of a room and about as much light as a 60-watt bulb.

ature extremes isn't often a matter of a single, crushing, attention-grabbing moment. Temperatures nonetheless present a pretty compelling level of danger when viewed in comparison to other disasters as shown through statistics.

Figures on deaths directly attributed to individual, severe weather events show heat waves have been more deadly in the United States than tornadoes in recent decades. From 1988 through 2011, stretches of excessive heat and humidity took an average of 146 lives per year. Tornadoes, meanwhile, took an average of 76 lives during each of those years, according to National Weather Service statistics.

Heat waves took nearly triple the toll on human lives than hurricanes did when viewed from that broader 24-year average. It might be a mind-boggling statistic at the surface. Memories, after all, tend to focus on events such as Hurricane Katrina or Superstorm Sandy. We lean on thoughts of all the devastation that reaches our homes through images on our computer and television screens. Hurricanes, though, when viewed over that wide-view, 24-year scale brought an average of only 56 annual deaths, the NWS reports.

Heat is a notable killer annually. Those living in or near Chicago wouldn't need a reminder on the toll that temperatures can take. A sweltering heat wave that struck the city in July 1995 caused more than 700 deaths.

Temperatures rose in excess of 100 degrees in the Windy City and elsewhere in the Upper Midwest. That stretch of heat was made all the more miserable by accompanying high humidity. More than 3,000 people in Chicago sought care in emergency rooms before the mercury on the thermometers began its merciful decline.

It was a crisis that might not have stuck to the country's collective memory in the same vein as so many others have. Heat waves, unlike hurricanes, aren't given first names. For a point of comparison, Hurricane Ike in 2008 was among America's most damaging in terms of property loss. Its irreplaceable toll was less so. It took 195 lives as it moved through the Caribbean, into the Gulf of Mexico and onward into Louisiana and Texas. That's less than a third of Chicago's 1995 losses from the all-important human standpoint.

That major heat wave, as well as its corresponding death toll, was far and away an anomaly. The human lives taken by heat in our country are more often spread thin across the summer months and among many different places. It's a danger that quietly comes to bear one death at a time. The prepper should take note. Those who don't pay close attention could lose track of some fairly significant risks.

Statistics tell the bigger story. The United States, believe it or not, is occasionally fortunate to have some years pass by without a single death attributable to a hurricane. There wasn't a single hurricane-related death in either 2006 or 2010, according to the weather service. Only one died from a hurricane in 2007. There were only two throughout 2009.

That simply isn't the case when it comes to extreme temperatures. In 2011, 29 deaths were attributed to cold weather events in the United States, according to the weather service. In 2010, 34 died from extreme cold events. In 2011, extreme high temperatures took 206 lives. Extreme heat brought 138 fatalities across the country the year before.

The statistical breakdown from one smaller angle speaks pretty loudly to the importance of what preppers need to accomplish through their planning. Though 21 of those who died from exposure to cold weather elements in 2011 were in an outdoor setting, six of those people died from cold weather while in their homes. More than half of the 206 who lost their lives to high heat events that year died inside their homes. The numbers go to show that preparedness from the perspective of shelter goes beyond having a roof and four walls to rely upon.

The skeptic might look at the mortality figures with little concern and question the need for preparing. Either side of the temperature scale does present an extremely low risk of death on a statistical basis when stacked against many other dangers that face us in our day-to-day lives. It's nonetheless important to recognize our vulnerabilities and have the ability to overcome them.

A prepper would look at the odds from a different perspective. Certainly, people are far more likely to die from a car crash than from extreme heat. Then again, most people are out and about on the roads for substantial periods on a daily basis. People are far more likely to die from a fire than from hypothermia. All of us, however, live in homes, work in buildings and drive in cars. Each carries a variety of fire risks.

A prepper's viewpoint on risks would be best served by accounting for that short, three-hour deadline as provided by the rule of threes. Extreme temperatures happen frequently enough. You fall to a severe disadvantage when either extreme is combined with an inability to escape. Shelter requires urgency. It makes the very best sense to have plans to eliminate a pressing and dangerous threat. The big-time hazards that accompany inadequate shelter are ultimately preventable for those who do their homework.

Surviving the elements

Shelter, just like every other piece of preparation, starts with listening to that strong voice of common sense that developed through all of our experiences. Each of us has a pretty firm understanding of "hot." Many of us know a pretty good thing or two about "cold." Simply living is enough to give most people some sense of the dangers at hand as it pertains to shelter needs.

Anyone who lives in a cold weather climate is all too familiar with the feeling of numb fingertips, stiff facial muscles and the burning sting that reminds you that those reddening ears have been uncovered for just a few minutes too long. Most anyone could remember a variety of moments of feeling thirsty, weary and maybe just "a bit off" while at work or engaged in play under that hot summer sun.

Problems most often grow from minor and manageable to severe and dangerous when people, for whatever reason, decide to ignore that "gut feeling" that something just isn't right. You should always take advantage of what the body has to say and with full urgency when it comes to shelter. The clock is already ticking toward that three-hour mark when the gut feeling starts talking to the mind. Those beyond the home or any adequate cool or warmth can't afford to waste a minute. Try to imagine the growing stress and the racing thoughts that would come should troubles grow from bad to worse when there's limited time and no adequate relief in sight.

Good shelter planning might begin outside of any concerns of disaster. It should be thought of from the perspective of basic survival. Those heading off from home should think ahead toward the possibility of an emergency and have some provisions to warm up or cool off along with them. Always think, "three hours." Ideas and the flexibility to improvise could, in some cases, make up for what you are lacking in gear.

It starts with communication. We're living in an era in which you can't escape from the barrage of messages. They come from those we know, from those we don't and whether they're wanted or not. Interestingly, valuable communication is still so often forgotten.

Hunters, fishermen, bikers, hikers or anyone else heading beyond the stretches of civilization should never forget to let someone know generally where they're heading and the time they intend upon returning. You should always meet those self-imposed deadlines regardless of how well the fish are biting or whether the biker's ambition is calling for those extra four miles. We've all heard about the boy who cries wolf. There's a good reason that story has held its lasting power. Your best chance of a prompt rescue when plans go awry is always left with friend or loved one before you head out onto the trail or into the field. Make sure someone knows when it's finally time to send out a search party. Make sure friends or family can take it seriously.

Accommodating the body's need for a balanced temperature could be met well through the contents of a prepper's go-bag. Those with a healthy respect for the rule of threes wouldn't travel far beyond the home without having their bags at hand. A good bag would account for shelter in several different ways.

My go-bag was very intentionally designed to recognize shelter's critical place in the rule of threes. Several shelter contingencies are kept in a pouch on the outside of the pack. In the event of an emergency, I wouldn't have to root through the entire bag to locate those items of most immediate need. My bag includes several ways to start a fire at close reach.

There's a poncho I could grab quickly if the clouds decided to open up and make life that much tougher. The contents of the bag include a change of warm, dry clothing. There's a tarp tucked inside and I have a small tent to provide some refuge from any potentially troublesome elements, whether it's cold winds, rain or the hot sun.

A go-bag goes a long way toward making life easier, but of course, that's assuming you thought your plan through and dutifully grabbed your gear before venturing out. Those who become caught in the elements without an assortment of supplies might have to revert to some childhood creativity. All of us growing up had the imagination to build all kinds of different forts and in many different ways.

The unprepared person who recognizes he's stuck and could be out there for a while might quickly gather up sticks and twigs and put up a lean-to as a way to at least keep dry should rain start to fall. Those caught out in the winter could buy some time and increase their chances with a snow shelter. A couple caught out in the rain with one poncho between them might stretch it out and run it among some branches to create a makeshift roof. Desperate times call for you to use some creativity.

Weather statistics pretty clearly suggest the risks brought by heat of summer or cold of winter extend beyond the unfortunate stuck in the wilderness or otherwise beyond places of regular refuge. Deaths occur in the middle of cities. It happens in homes.

Risks carried by extreme temperatures would only grow for those struggling during periods of disaster recovery. It's elementary. Those who experienced home damage or destruction would face greater exposure to the elements. Those who haven't planned ahead are stuck with what they're given.

Superstorm Sandy provided a noteworthy example. Several of the more than 200 deaths caused by the major Atlantic storm were attributed to hypothermia. If the storm wasn't damaging enough, those in its path were put at further danger by its unfortunate timing.

The storm made landfall on the East Coast in the latter days of October, when fall's chill had already taken firm grasp on the Northeast. Plummeting temperatures followed quickly

behind. Flooding was an issue of serious concern. The power outages that stretched across the region became a more pressing matter upon forecasts of snow, high winds and cold.

The risk of hypothermia was enough of a concern after Sandy that New York Mayor Michael

It would be wise for a family to keep several Aladdin lamps around the home to account for light and a means to pick up the temperature in a blackout situation.

Bloomberg issued a warning and detailed the symptoms those suffering might experience. Vast numbers had little access to heat. The American Red Cross picked up its efforts in providing additional shelters and distributing blankets to those in need.

Preparing for and getting through a stay-in-place, cold weather emergency should start with recognition that gas and electrical hook-ups haven't been around forever. People throughout history made it through the worst weather that nature could bring.

Those of us living today can do the same, but we could better do so by envisioning the misery of having to get through unprepared. Listen to the gut and get the right backups in place.

The furnace is a wonderful and often reliable appliance, but it's nonetheless one that's far too often taken for granted. Those who live in climates that experience below-freezing temperatures for nearly half of the calendar

A wood stove and an ample food supply can make a disaster situation comfortable for weeks.

year might re-assess the wisdom of relying on a single tool to provide for adequate warmth and safety. It might not be a matter of disaster. Machines fall into disrepair. The one major snowstorm that knocks out the substation could just as quickly remind families of the need for a back-up plan.

Better yet, those folks should take initiative and consider their options before any winter event cuts off their gas or electricity. A boxer wouldn't require a punch to the face to know the wisdom of putting up some guard. Many of the provisions families could take to keep the family safe in such circumstances make good sense and for reasons well beyond the scope of preparedness. Winter can be a drain on the wallet. It's less so for homes that are properly put together to account for the cold.

Assuring the home has a good degree of insulation would keep the heat inside and the cold beyond its walls. Every degree of heat within would be important should a family lose its furnace at a time of need. It's a project that stands to save a family some significant money through even the calmest of winters. The furnace doesn't have to work as hard if the house isn't so quickly giving up all the warmth the furnace produces.

It's a shame that fireplaces are less often included in newly built homes. They provide a great source of heat and a cozy gathering point for the family. A fireplace certainly could become an option for some of those living in homes without. Many, though, might find themselves limited by finances or the lack of any good wall place that could accommodate one.

Wood stoves would also take some effort and investment, but they are often far more feasible than the traditional fireplace. They're functional. It's a matter of warmth before décor. A stove would certainly provide a great deal of warmth to a home, whether during an outage or otherwise.

Many people have invested in the more modern pellet stoves. They burn compressed wood. They do so efficiently and without a lot of mess or effort. Models are available that would open the option to those with even the smallest of homes. You could purchase a window-mount model that's no different size-wise than the room air conditioners so many have. They're options that would take some spending on the front end, but they would also come to save the family some money in the long run. When used regularly, traditional wood stoves and pellet stoves of any type would take some of the heating burden off of the furnace.

Those who aren't in the right place to make a big initial investment in a good secondary heat source could still assemble smaller and less pricy options to provide a little warmth should Mother Nature put the family in a tough spot. Buddy heaters, which operate on propane, are safe for indoor use in an emergency and would give the family the ability to warm up a room. They typically sell for about $100. Smaller models run less. The bigger models with all the bells and whistles would cost more.

I previously mentioned Aladdin lamps as a contingency I enjoy as a matter of function and décor. It's a tool that goes back more than a century. It played a big role in American life in the era just before electrical power became commonplace in the average home.

The technology might be antiquated when viewed against all our modern wonders, but there's little better to have in the home when electricity fails and a family is stuck with the capabilities that their ancestors had 100 years back. It's a great light source. An Aladdin lamp would provide 60 watts of light. It's enough for you to see your way around. They provide some good reading light. For preppers, it offers much more. One Aladdin lamp provides 2,200 BTUs of heat. It's enough warmth to take the chill off of a 10-by-10 room.

Aladdin lamps are still manufactured and out there in the market-

place. You might also keep watch at flea markets, garage sales or second-hand stores. The antique versions are bound to look nicer and would likely come at a lesser expense. The lamp that's a century old will still work and offer the same level of function as the new

If you find yourself lost, you only have a short time to decide if you need a fire and shelter. Making the wrong choice could put you in a very serious situation.

model just unpacked from its box. Any family would be wise to have several around the home to account for light and a means to pick up the temperature.

Those left in the cold, whether prepared or not, shouldn't panic regardless of how bitter the outdoor temperatures have become. The home might lose some comfort, but it would remain a viable refuge from however cold it is outdoors. Those without the right tools would have a tougher time, but it would take some time before survival becomes an issue.

A home's temperature would decline, but at a fairly slow pace. One of the bigger considerations in a cold weather emergency would go beyond issues comfort and safety. If you don't have a back-up heat source, you would want to take the steps necessary to assure the pipes don't burst. Should cold persist, you would want to shut down the water and then drain off what's left inside. It would often take a couple of weeks of pretty miserable temperatures to reach that point.

In a cold weather emergency, families should take advantage of the best they have. The sun is a tremendous source of heat. Opening up the shades would allow the sunshine to provide for some warmth. It's often enough to raise the home's temperature by a few degrees.

Those who live in the colder weather zones would most certainly have some contingencies at the ready whether or not they're preppers. Any of those folks would be bound to have some long underwear, a good supply of heavy sweatshirts and some warm blankets at quick reach. It would suffice for survival, if not for comfort.

If you're stuck without shelter and could be there for a while, a lean-to will at least keep you dry should rain or snow start to fall.

Those struggling through the cold would need to keep some basic safety considerations in mind. Charcoal is certainly a tremendous and inexpensive heat source common to most households, though it's never to be burned inside the home. The risk of carbon monoxide poisoning would put the family at far greater risk than would any temperature regardless of how uncomfortable anyone is becoming. Those completely helpless to temperature would die in three hours. Carbon monoxide poisoning could kill within minutes. Generators are never to be used in the home and for the very same reason.

Those who live in cold weather climates would want to extend shelter planning to their cars. Many of us spend good periods of our days on the road. Of course, any good prepper would have his go-bag in the backseat. There are, however, several other tools you would want to have stowed in the trunk in addition that could lessen the chances shelter would become an issue. Those driving in snow or on ice are always at a good risk of going off the road. Those driving in rural areas could face the risk of being stuck there for some time.

Motorists should keep a snow shovel in the trunk. Road salt, sand or cat litter is an important pack-away. You could put it under and around the tires to offer some trac-tion. On occasion, those tools just aren't enough.

You should have some road flares to serve as a beacon to others. In recognizing the importance of self-reliance, you would keep a set of jumper cables and a tow chain in the trunk. You couldn't guarantee that any Good Samaritan that stops by would have the right tools for the job. In a tough situation, it's always blessing enough to see someone who's ready and willing to help.

A prepper should make good use of space. The greater challenge of a go-bag is putting together a package that's lightweight, compact and meets the rule of threes. The bag probably wouldn't hold a sleeping bag. The trunk or back seat of any vehicle certainly would. You could survive with less, but you can never underestimate the power of any bit of comfort during a difficult situation.

Preppers who anticipate challenges can often avoid them. A good prepper should always keep the gas tank full whether it's warm or cold. Those with a lesser degree of vigilance who drive in winter weather should know they're setting themselves up for big trouble by letting the gas tank fall below half. The car or truck isn't going to move if the fuel lines are frozen.

Good shelter, as it pertains to heat concerns, can get a bit trickier when viewed from a disaster situation. You could hope a disaster wouldn't happen in conjunction with temperatures of 100 degrees or more. Preppers, however, don't rely on hope. You might not be able to avoid the heat. You could all the same maintain health and safety.

Those in short-term situations or otherwise on the front-end of a disaster might rely on an easy solution. A prepper might determine that fans or air conditioners during extreme circumstances would take priority when drawing from the power available from the generator. Those experiencing a heat wave on the tail-end of a longer-term recovery might not have the gas available to keep that generator running.

You could then rely on a variety of methods beyond those that require electricity to keep the family safe. Again, people didn't always have those tools to rely upon. Our forefathers made it through the hottest, most miserable of days. So can those of us living today.

Simple science provides some

possibilities. Just as it's wise to open the shades for the sun's warmth in winter's cold, it's just as smart to pull them closed on the hottest days. We all know that heat rises. Those with nothing else might find some bit of relief by sticking to the lowest floors of the home. Those who have basements could set up living spaces and ride out a heat wave down there.

Pay attention to all of the things that could add heat to the home. The unbearable 100-degree day isn't the best time to turn the oven on for a few hours of baking. Some examples are less obvious.

Many people, for instance, crank open their windows on the hot days in the hopes of catching some breeze from time to time. It might sound strange, but you would do more harm than good in doing so during the daytime. Those who have

Those who experience home damage or destruction in a disaster face greater exposure to the elements. Preppers can plan ahead so they avoid living in situations like this tent city in Haiti following the 2010 earthquake there.

an indoor temperature that's lesser than that of the outside air would only serve to let more heat into the home. You could rely on that breeze and some ventilation when the sun falls and temperatures drop if only even slightly during the overnight hours.

Methods of maintaining proper cool in the hottest of temperatures would go well beyond the home itself. You should be mindful of your body's needs and place proper priority on temperature when it's due. It's wise to limit physical exertion at the hottest times of the day. Of course, recovery takes work. It can still be accomplished with strategy that keeps safety and welfare at the forefront. At a time of dangerous temperatures, all of those tasks that come to bear during a disaster aftermath might be better accomplished in the earliest hours of morning or the late hours of evening. It might be smarter to get your rest in during the hottest hours that come in mid to late afternoon.

Those who are living through extreme heat would need to drink a lot of fluids. Water needs would be far greater than what a person would consume on the average day. You shouldn't wait until you're thirsty.

Water is a tremendous resource for cooling in ways beyond hydration. Those who can't power up the air conditioner could cool their bodies with cold baths and showers at several points during the day. In between, you might keep the skin dampened with a towel. The water's evaporation from the skin, in the same fashion as sweat, would serve to cool the body.

It's also important to recognize that the elderly are far more vulnerable to death in extreme heat. More than 43 percent of heat-related fatalities in 2011 involved people who were age 70 or older. More than 79 percent of deaths caused by extreme heat involved people who were age 50 and older, according to the weather service. Youth, it seems, is one of the best defenses against extreme heat as it comes to survival. People younger than age 30 accounted for less than 4 percent of the heat-related deaths that year.

Part of your plan for getting through the hottest of days should include acting as a compassionate neighbor. If you live nearby to an elderly resident, you might stop by and check up from time to time to make sure the heat isn't taking a toll. It wouldn't have to be a disaster situation. If you know the elderly couple down the street doesn't have air conditioning, you might stop by for visits on the hottest days of summer to account for their wellbeing. Those who understand the dangers should take

Hygiene is an area of preparation you can't afford to overlook. Biological functions aren't going to take a furlough for reasons of inconvenience. Having the means to get the grime off of your body is a morale and confidence builder, and both are important in times of challenge. Further, it's a health issue.

Alcohol-based hand sanitizers have been a big trend of recent years. The sanitizers are everywhere, and they're better than nothing. Still, you shouldn't rely on them as the overriding hygiene prep. From the place of practicality, sanitizers might kill some germs, but they aren't going to remove the filth. Bath-in-a-bag kits are handy and work well, though many do not have to take on that additional expense. There's really nothing better than the regular standbys — soap and water.

A family might not have showers available if a storm knocks the community off the municipal water system or inhibits the ability to draw from the well. Some might have adequate water storage to dedicate a portion for hygiene. Those who don't can still most often meet needs. With the exception of those living in the desert, most people have fairly close access to water. Though you wouldn't drink directly from a lake, river or stream, that water might just suffice for washing up.

Use some forethought, common sense and good judgment. If the only nearby water source is the filthy, contaminated harbor, you might think better of collecting from it for hygiene purposes. In that

Hand sanitizer is better than nothing, but it won't remove the filth you'll encounter in a disaster area.

Pre-moistened towelettes can help remove some grime from your body in a disaster situation.

case, have those bath kits ready. Those using untreated water for washing would want to take greater care. While working in New Orleans after Hurricane Katrina, we had access to our showers, but had untreated water flowing through the pipes. I felt comfortable in using that water for showering from the shoulders down. I wouldn't, however, use it to brush my teeth as some did. I relied on bottled water to cleanse my face and ears. I didn't want to risk giving contaminants any easy entry point that could lead to illness.

Toilet access would become an issue should a family lose typical water access. One solution might be a five-gallon pail and commode seat. Preps might include waste alleviation and gelling bags, which are also referred to as WAG bags. The bags contain a material that neutralizes odors and speeds the decay process. They're sealable and can be deposited in the trash. Depending on the length of time before water is restored, it could be a somewhat pricey option. They typically sell for a few dollars apiece.

There are a variety of chemical camping toilets on the market at a wide range of prices. They're basically smaller, personal versions of the portable bathrooms you would see at festivals or on construction sites. Of course, those with fewer hang-ups with their daily functions could get by with a shovel.

Consider personal comfort and that of the family members. It'll provide the best guide to most adequate solutions.

some degree of responsibility to watch out for those vulnerable folks who might not.

Shelter for those bugging out would require all the same thoughts and concerns applicable to body temperature. Those who properly planned and executed an evacuation would have little concern. They were able to quickly assemble and pack their necessities. They're away from danger and making a temporary home at one of their pre-determined places, whether it's a loved one's home or a hotel room.

Families who are bugging out under less coordinated circumstances would have a few additional things to think about. It might take a few more thoughts from the more commonly recognized idea of shelter, which would include some degree of security. A variety of circumstances could put families on the move. It could be the family with the best preps and a good ability to camp out in place. They might be forced from their neighborhood because of a gas leak. A broken water main could flood out a neighborhood if crews are too busy to offer prompt response.

Those forced from the home with a tent and some supplies would want to find an adequately safe spot to set up their camp. Exercise common sense. Those in a coastal area could find a better spot than ocean side at low tide. You wouldn't pitch a tent anywhere near a distressed levy. It makes a lot of sense to find a spot away from any environmental dangers and subtle enough to avoid the dangers of other people.

Those making camp would want to consider ways to protect themselves and their supplies. Those who have dogs have great alarms right within their family units.

A dog is often enough to scare off those intent on theft. Motion detecting alarms come cheap, and you could pack it in with the camping gear so it's always ready to go.

All of the areas pertaining to shelter come down to forethought and appropriate respect for the potential troubles out there. When it comes to preparing, shelter is no different than any other component of the plan. It's always a matter of thinking ahead and getting to work. When it comes to the rule of threes, shelter is far different. Those who didn't finish their homework have little time to make it right when the emergency is finally at hand. Shelter is definitely job No. 1.

If you are forced to live in a tent, put it up away from any environmental dangers and in a place where you can avoid the dangers of other people.

7

GUNS AND AMMO

These are some of
the author's tools
for self-defense.

It's easy to take for granted the men and women who provide law enforcement during typical times when everything is right with the world. Even in the best times, everyone faces some risk of victimization. Crimes happen every day. Still, most people appropriately take a good degree of comfort that law enforcement — with its

full range of capabilities — is rarely more than a phone call and just a few minutes from response.

The community takes great ease in knowing officers are patrolling the streets and are on the lookout for suspicious activity. With the help of the community's eyes, police can occasionally stop crimes as they're occurring. The mere presence of a skilled police force is often enough to give second thoughts to some of those with ill intentions. Disaster is different.

Police officers and sheriff's deputies provide among the most vital of community services, and I'm proud to have a role in that profession. Communities, however, don't fund police departments with the very worst-case scenarios in mind. Though departments plan well and build great contingencies, catastrophe can quickly compromise any community's ability to properly ensure public safety.

Part of preparing means thinking about how to manage and provide for personal safety when the typical level of public protection just isn't possible. People might need to protect themselves. Carrying a firearm and having proper ammunition makes a lot of sense for a post-disaster recovery. It actually makes just as much sense for the typical day.

It's important to note that disaster situations most often lend to environments in which the community rallies together and works for the greater good. People most often look out for each other. Disasters, however, also give rise to opportunists who recognize a chance to profit from the disorder. Periods of civil unrest have been noted. You can't ignore the lesser protections available to the community when disasters strain the system.

Even in the best of times, there are thousands of people to every single officer on patrol. Our system of law and order relies on the premise that accidents and difficulties are very rare on a daily basis. It counts on the fact that typically only a very small few of our citizens are engaging in criminal activity. A disaster situation can shift things.

I carry a firearm every day. I do so recognizing that even a 911 call would be too little and too late when a dire threat is staring right into my eyes. Any number of examples illustrates that risk.

News reports have highlighted violent struggles recorded by dispatchers that ended up being homicide scenes by the time police arrived. The mass shootings in the United States in recent years illustrate the speed by which violent episodes unfold. Though police arrived quickly, they arrived to several deaths. Carrying a gun is part of how I live. I don't expect to encounter a violent episode that

would threaten my life on any given day, though I surely wouldn't want be without it should any life-threatening circumstance arise.

I'd suggest the United States would be safer if all honest, law-abiding citizens carried firearms. It's valuable to disaster preparation when considering how much the landscape can change amid chaos. Several factors could open a greater-than-usual possibility of violence.

The priorities of police agencies expand as a wide range of new problems emerge. Police officers are relied upon as life savers and are appropriately pulled into search-and-rescue roles to bring the injured to safety. Officers would have a role in general community safety. They'd still have their role in response to criminal activity, which could become a bigger issue than usual.

In a self-defense situation, the idea is not to start a war, just to end the fight.

The everyday law-abiding citizen stands a greater chance of finding himself in a hapless situation in a disaster scenario. The most severe of situations would get immediate attention from a stretched-thin police force. Some calls that would otherwise have been considered serious that would have drawn prompt response might simply have to wait. Police could no longer patrol up and down the nighttime streets if they're required on specific calls. A community's public safety efforts, those built for the typical day, can become overloaded in very short order.

The daunting workload required from police agencies in the wake of disaster is just part of the issue. Disasters could mean direct impacts on those departments as well as on the men and women who work for them. Police departments aren't indestructible castles with ultimate protection from the elements. Departments would have to press through and make the best with less should a disaster destroy equipment.

Individual officers are real-life people like anyone else. When the shift is over and it's time to change out of their uniforms, they head home to their families. They, too, experience their own losses amid catastrophe and have their own loved ones and a host of worries at the fronts of their minds. They have to manage all those thoughts while still trying to give their best to a community in need. When the community at large is dealing with chaos, members of law enforcement might often deal with stress at a far higher degree.

In some cases, after disaster or otherwise, there's no time to wait for assistance. In many violent,

life-threatening situations, the very best police officers can do is react and investigate in the aftermath. Disasters create a new environment. Many people become desperate. The criminal element might recognize a lesser likelihood of legal repercussions given all that police already have on their hands.

Readiness is never a matter of expecting the worst, but it accounts for the possibility. No one can predict if a disaster would bring out the community's best, lead to social disorder or present elements of both. One thing is inevitable: those dedicated to public safety couldn't possibly offer the same impact in the early hours after a disaster, whether from positions of crime prevention or prompt reaction.

Those aiming to protect themselves in an environment of heightened vulnerability have several considerations to make. An easy, common-sense measure of self-protection is simply keeping low-key and limiting the likelihood that criminals would identify a person or the family home as a profitable, potential target. When thinking about the worst-case scenario — a life-threatening confrontation — having the right firearms becomes an appropriate part of your planning efforts.

Police officers had a vital role in the aftermath of Hurricane Katrina, but in some areas and for a

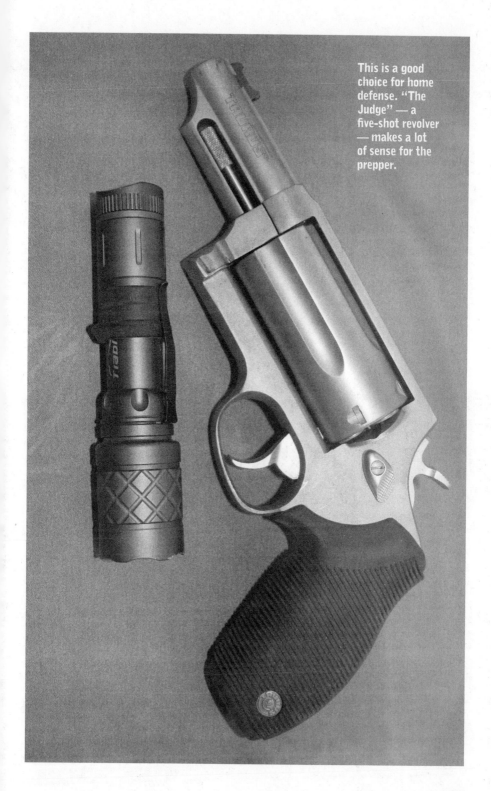

This is a good choice for home defense. "The Judge" — a five-shot revolver — makes a lot of sense for the prepper.

variety of reasons, they couldn't possibly fulfill needs on their own. Capabilities were severely diminished. Police lost vehicles and equipment to the hurricane. A communications blackout in New Orleans hampered efforts to assemble even a serviceable level of coordination. Some officers there failed to show for duty, putting further stress on the men and women who took on those enormous tasks.

Attention and effort was split between search and rescue and

maintaining order in the early hours after the disaster. At some level, that major American city devolved into a state of anarchy. A few days after landfall, most of the officers in the New Orleans Police Department were pulled off of res-

cue operations in effort to pull the city back from the criminal element.

It speaks loudly to the impact crime can

If the tactical flavor is more for your taste, black guns are very practical and readily available.

have after disaster. Every officer that was reassigned to handle looters and other lawlessness was an officer that couldn't be out there looking for the elderly, disabled and injured. National Guard units and private security operations mobilized quickly. It was a sad state of affairs all the same.

You could draw some distinctions, of course. You could hold lesser animosity for the people in a state of panic who stole groceries and other provisions out of survival fears. You might have fewer problems with a family that climbed through the broken window and into the shoe store to put new pairs on each of their children after flooding washed away their belongings.

It's something completely different when you consider those who loaded up on new furniture, expensive booze, big-screen televisions and other luxuries in the wake of all the chaos. There were plenty of the latter. Many businesses were cleared out to their walls, and plenty of those goods went well beyond the realm of necessities.

Regaining a sense of order was no easy task. Officers had to prioritize who they were hauling in, and in many cases, police were limited to a system of catch and release. The jail sustained significant damage in the hurricane, leaving the capacity to house offenders at a high premium. It meant law enforcement simply let go many of those causing trouble unless they were involved in violent offenses. Rampant crime not only affected the crucial work of rescuing those from the floodwaters, but it also stood in the way of those who came in to start repairs on the power grid and other infrastructure.

Though Hurricane Katrina was a unique situation in so many ways,

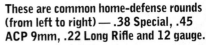

These are common home-defense rounds (from left to right) — .38 Special, .45 ACP 9mm, .22 Long Rifle and 12 gauge.

it stands as a firm example of why preparation is so important. It isn't the only example. Reports of looting began to pile up in and near New York City in 2012 after Superstorm Sandy cleared. It isn't solely a modern phenomenon. Looting and crime were rampant following the major hurricane that battered New England in September 1938.

The hurricane came prior to our modern practice of assigning first names to storms, though it came to be known by many as "The Long Island Express" based on its landfall there on Sept. 21, 1938. Many take the advances in weather forecasting and storm tracking that most often provide modern society adequate means to take precaution for granted. New England was blindsided by the storm, which stood among the very worst disasters of the 20th century. The hurricane touched 10 New England states before finally falling apart in southern Quebec, Canada.

The Express left several hundred dead in its wake and caused $4.7 billion in damage by modern, monetary figures. Mobs then, like the mobs in modern times, took full advantage of the disorder. It's pertinent to consider the timeframe. The hurricane wreaked its havoc amid the Great Depression, and desperation was already at a fevered pitch when the Express rolled through.

Certainly, you couldn't generalize or pin specific motives on lawbreakers as a whole, whether thinking of long ago or during more recent history. Some might have stolen for survival then. Some might have stolen for survival in 2005 and 2012. Some certainly had profit in mind. Authorities in some locales following the 1938 storm were given "shoot to kill" orders in efforts to restore safety and security among the chaos. Fast-forward 68 years, and police in the wake of Katrina received those same orders.

Some have claimed the modern era is far less civil than past generations. The criminal behavior at play in 1938 and again in the 21st century suggests it isn't a matter of the era. Those building their preparedness plans might note that those who ignore history are doomed to repeat it.

Remember that preparation isn't an act in pessimism. Research has shown that, in general, lawlessness is a phenomenon of the very few in the aftermath of any disaster situation. It stands to reason. The vast majority of people typically live within the lines of the law regardless of any everyday opportunities.

It is positive to note that most, according to research, tend to get through disasters and their aftermaths and onto the task of rebuilding without experiencing criminal harm. Preparedness, however, calls for you to take note of the anecdotal evidence. A crime victim wouldn't take solace that his robbery was one of just a few in an overall safe recovery period.

Disasters have sparked unrest, and it's clear that community resources lack their common effectiveness in a chaotic environment. It's worth a bet on the side of safety should circumstances create a risk that you could fall on the wrong side of the statistics. Preparation efforts now might better assure the activities of even a limited number of people wouldn't open your family to inescapable difficulties.

Assessing our needs

Gun ownership is another area that tends to show people truly are far better off to live as they prepare. Firearms aren't a tool you should buy only to tuck away for "just in case" possibilities. As much as guns would provide a layer of safety in troubled times, they're available as a means of protection every day of the week. Those unfamiliar with guns would have to put in a fair amount of work. A person who has never fired a gun couldn't expect to make any good use of it in an emergency.

Firearms are a more complex piece of the overall planning puzzle. Beyond guns and ammunition, being properly prepared requires having the proper mindset to meet the challenge of a life-threatening situation. To put it bluntly, having guns at the ready for safety in a disaster's aftermath is preparing for a moment where it's kill or be killed.

There isn't a book, a video or a training course that could get you into the state of mind you'd need to come through on the other side. It's very personal. You would have to ask yourself whether you'd be able to take another person's life if violently threatened in a confrontation.

Amid that type of confrontation, a person doesn't shoot to wound. You would only put yourself at more risk by pulling a firearm as a bluff with hope it's enough to get the bad guys running. Those who pull a gun in self-defense when violently confronted shoot to kill. It's a heavy thought for many to weigh.

Often, people find the right strength, courage and determination inside of themselves when confronted with such a dire moment. It's all the same worth thinking about. It goes to show the type of gun you carry is far less meaningful than the efforts and strategies you take to avoid threats. The firearm is always the option of last resort.

Having a gun means being ready for that situation where no other options exist. When it comes to choosing guns, realize there aren't one or two generic, perfect firearms on the market that'll meet everyone's general needs. The types of firearms to assemble from the standpoints of safety and preparedness will depend on factors including your familiarity with guns, preference of firearms and how much you are willing to spend.

You should think about how the gun or guns would be used. An avid hunter might choose differently than someone who is solely concerned about protection. Gun enthusiasts often spend more than others, because beyond hunting or personal protection, it's a hobby and a collection they enjoy. For some people out there, a firearm's value extends no further than its utility. There are plenty of firearms to meet needs along the full range of interests and reasons for purchase.

The hobbyist who shoots regularly might consider a civilian-version M4 semi-automatic rifle. It's a re-ally nice firearm, and if spending is no option, a light and a holographic sight would make for nice add-ons. Price on that gun is a key factor to think about.

Even a basic setup could be enough to dissuade the cost-conscious non-collectors who are looking for no more than a means to protect their homes or persons. A bare-bones model is going to run $800 or more. The buyers would still need to open their wallets a little wider for ammo magazines and other accessories.

Big gun enthusiasts also sometimes lean toward the Russian AK models. They're pretty handy and work in all conditions. The ammo is also fairly inexpensive.

Those who want to protect their homes without spending the big dollars have any number of options. There are a variety of nice home-defense shotguns on the market in the $500 range. Examples would include the Mossberg 500 and 590 models, the Winchester Model 12, Winchester's stainless steel 1300 Marine model and the Remington H70. As for handguns, Glock's .45-caliber and 9mm pistols are tough to beat.

The M1 carbine is a nice personal protection gun. It's a short firearm when compared against shotguns. It's easy to handle and it'll offer better range than a pistol.

Ammunition is a tougher consideration to weigh. There's really no firm round count you should have on hand. Like other pieces of preparation, it comes down to the depth of preparedness you seek and your personal comfort level.

Those planning to survive the end of civilization as we know it would probably want a few thousand rounds for every gun in the battery. Most, however, wouldn't think that far ahead and need that kind of stockpile. I have a couple of 12-gauge shotguns in the house for defensive purposes. I probably keep a couple hundred rounds of buckshot and a couple hundred slugs handy at any given time.

Both would meet the needs of protection. It opens another point for thought. At a very general level, the best prepared are able to get several functions out of many of their various tools. Guns fit well into that mold.

Should a disaster set up a

U.S. Military surplus ammo cans work perfectly for what they were designed for — long-term ammunition storage.

long-term recovery effort, firearms might also become part of food plans. Buckshot or slugs would work well for personal protection, but they would also open the door to hunting deer or other large game. I'd also suggest keeping some 4 shot or 7 shot among the ammunition supply for hunting birds, squirrels or other small game in the event sustenance requires.

Merely having a gun and a supply of ammo shouldn't be enough to make you comfortable. Those who own them need to get out and use them. Think about it another way: having a full pantry of good ingredients doesn't make you a chef. Firearms only work best in the hands of capable operators.

An owner should feel comfortable with how his guns fire. Gun owners should spend some time at the range or out in the field and develop some skill. A good level of proficiency is important. Defining proficiency, however, is another area like so many in the realm of preparation where no one can really offer any true, reliable benchmarks.

According to the old saying, you should "beware of the man who only has one gun." If he only has one, you can rest assured he's going to know how to use it. Taking it another next step forward, they say, "beware of the man who only has a single-shot gun." He's the man who's really going to know what he's doing. They wouldn't have become old sayings if they didn't carry some truth.

For the purposes of preparedness, proficiency is only the first figure in the overall safety equation. Though skill has a role in preparedness, it's empty without the determination to overcome crisis. There's only one important standard to assess as to whether abilities fall into the right place amid violent confrontations. If a person is standing across from a criminal pointing a gun with a finger on the trigger, which of the two is going to walk away?

If you're relatively new to firearms, you would want to think about your skills and familiarity with your gun in determining your comfort in carrying for personal protection. It's certainly important to practice. There are a variety of firearm training courses out there that start at very basic levels, move onto more advanced skills and address different topics. They might hold value for some gun owners.

You should never let training obscure the ultimate goal of personal protection though. Winning is everything, and the means of victory don't matter. When the final bullet of a violent confrontation is fired, it's a matter of being dead or alive. At the end of the day, the right mindset and mental toughness —

the ability to manage through crisis and handle that adrenaline rush — are far more important than accuracy. A life-threatening event is an extreme mental challenge. It isn't a sharpshooting event.

As for proficiency, you shouldn't find yourself fumbling with your gun. You should be able to promptly reload. It's a matter of having enough skill and comfort with a gun to assure the bad guy can't take advantage of any shortcomings.

On the converse, you don't have to score a 100 on a sniper test or obliterate the middle of any targets while out on the range. I've known a number of police officers through the years who aren't the most accurate of shooters but are, all the same, well prepared for their duties. It's only about winning.

The idea is illustrated in a recent story of a gun shop owner in the South who encountered three armed men intent on robbing his place. It quickly escalated. The store owner was threatened and recognized he would've been killed if he hadn't relied on his gun and fired. One of the robbers died on site.

The two others escaped from the shop, though they were caught down the road just minutes later with critical injuries. They were bleeding out. It's a story that demonstrates the importance of carrying but also lends to the greater point on proficiency. Escaping deadly situations with our lives is the only goal.

Soon after, an expert marksman and trainer with a list of credentials as long as his arm offered his thoughts on the encounter. It was a bit infuriating. Training would tell us to put two shots in the chest and a third in the head when thrust into an armed confrontation. Relying on that guideline, the trainer had sharp criticism for the storeowner for his lack of precision in having fired off more than two dozen rounds when fending off his attackers.

Guidelines are precisely that and lose significance when faced with the stark reality of a life-threatening encounter. The storeowner might not have met a trainer's definition of success, yet by a greater measure, he handled his crisis perfectly. He's lived to tell the tale.

You could find dozens upon dozens of stories highlighting the importance of firearms for personal protection. Familiarity with your gun is the first step. It's also important to have a solid understanding of laws regarding gun use. Across the country, there are a variety of different requirements in place for those who conceal weapons. You should research state requirements and get a permit for carry if the law requires.

There's a growing movement for uniformity and less restriction for concealed carry. While strides have been made, the United States is still patchwork when it comes to gun laws, and those differences could become important. Those traveling should pay keen attention to the concealed carry laws of the states to which they're heading.

A number of states offer reciprocity, or rather, allow the ability to carry a concealed weapon with a home-state permit or other means of showing compliance of your home state's laws. Keeping on the right side of the law only takes a few minutes of research. An Internet search would avail you to all of the information on restrictions, requirements and how reciprocity applies throughout the country.

It's also wise to have a base of knowledge on state laws regarding self-defense. Some states give residents greater leeway and the benefit of the doubt when they're pushed to use force in the midst of a threat. Many states rely on the castle doctrine, which allows for self-defense at home and doesn't obligate a resident to attempt

The author keeps an ample supply of 9mm ammo on hand at his home.

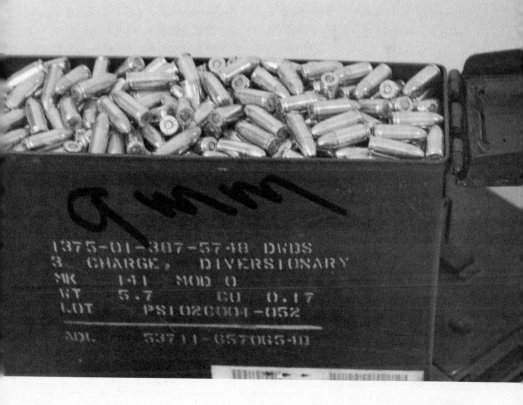

retreat before using force should someone break in. Other states have adopted stand-your-ground laws, which apply to wherever a person might be. They allow people to exercise force without an attempt at escape if a person reasonably believes he or she is facing harm.

Safety is a critical factor to think about in regard to firearms, and in ways some people might fail to consider. The means of concealing a weapon is an important safety consideration. You might feel safer in merely carrying a gun, but if it isn't well hidden, having a gun could actually open the door to big risks. There's very good reason to conceal firearms rather than wear them in plain view. Purchasing appropriate holsters and having the right attire should be just as much a part of the preparation plan as the pistols themselves.

A lot of people haven't thought that far. Many people out there are carrying their guns in those 5.11 tactical vests. They're the vests that look similar to what you'd see photographers wearing while out on a job assignment. Let's think about that holstering choice from a place of danger though. Concealed carry is important because you wouldn't want to advertise your ability to protect yourself and others should violence erupt. It's one thing to wear that type of vest as part of a security detail when it's already well evident what the person is doing and why he's in place. It's another thing for the average citizen going about his day that happens to have the means to put a quick end to a violent outburst.

Criminals carry guns for a specific reason. It creates fear and provides all the force they'll need to get precisely what they want. If, for instance, you went into a convenience store and an armed robber followed behind, having a gun that wasn't properly concealed would be akin to wearing a T-shirt that says, "I have a gun. Shoot me first." The tactical vest is a clear giveaway.

Try to be discreet. When I dress in the morning, I think about what gun I'm going to carry and what I'm going to wear that'll give me a low profile. People passing by would have no idea. That's the goal. Chances are pretty good that any one of us will make it through our typical days without any reason for worries. Should you find yourself in danger, it isn't advisable to have a target on your back or anything that serves as an overhead sign with an arrow pointing down that says, "This guy has a gun."

Safety is also an issue at home, particularly so for those who have children. The degree to which safety becomes an issue on the home front might differ depending on the ages of those children, their knowledge and the respect the kids hold for the power of firearms and their potential for danger. In that respect, there are two ways to address safety.

The simple, foolproof solution would be gun locks. Some would question whether it's the best answer when stacked against the very reason to have our firearms at reach. If an attacker breaks into your home and charges forward with a knife, you might not want to test your dexterity and wherewithal in removing that lock with sufficient time for protection.

I'd argue the better means of safety is taking all the necessary time and effort to teach children properly. I raised three children.

I had guns throughout the home, and we never had an issue. Moms and dads should show children what guns can do and make it abundantly clear that guns aren't toys. Talk about the guns and impart some respect for them. Those who try to keep the guns stowed away and out of reach only serve to build more potentially dangerous curiosity.

When the children are old enough to handle guns, it's time to teach them how to shoot so they get a better sense of firearms and why they need to be respected. It might be another of those many

In the author's opinion, the most cost-effective round — pound for pound — is .22 LR.

examples of how we've changed as generations have passed, but I can remember going out alone to hunt small game when I was a kid, probably no older than 9 years old .

Teaching children and keeping solid lines of communication open is the very essence of good parenthood. It makes sense that the same strategies would extend to firearms. It's an opportunity that could go beyond child safety to a better prepared household. It isn't inconceivable, after all, that an older child or young teen would be put in the position to defend the family from an attack.

Be smart, stay safe

A firearm is truly the one tool among a multi-faceted preparation plan that you hope is never needed. When you draw a firearm, you do so with intent to pull the trigger. Occasionally, the scare factor might defuse the crisis. Some crooks might not expect or want a battle. Chances, though, can't be taken when lives are on the line.

Shootings aren't justifiable when those threatened are merely uncomfortable by their situations. It's only legitimate to draw a weapon when the mind, with full clarity, determines that there is no other way out. A shooting is justified when you are truly and honestly in fear for your life. It's that moment where there is no longer any way to get around it. There's no negotiation.

That moment might rise when you have a firearm sighted at your head or chest. It might be a situation when a shot has already been fired. A bullet coming from the other direction makes a distinct sound that most are fortunate to never hear.

It might not be a firearm threat.

It could be a person struggling with a huge raging man using furniture or whatever else as weapons. The victim might realize the attacker isn't going to stop. Those put in the position of life-threatening harm will know it. It's a feeling and an understanding that words can't adequately describe.

The best option for those who find themselves in the midst of civil unrest after disaster is to do all possible to limit the possibility of being targeted for crime. Those who'd use their firearms in the midst of turmoil would have a new set of difficult issues after their attackers go down. A

The author says "it's hard to beat" his day-hiking rig — a Ruger .22.

confrontation might be a matter of moments, but the aftermath could continue for some time and carry all sorts of stress, even if you were fully justified in firing.

Those who properly defend themselves would still very likely end up in handcuffs and behind the cages of the squad cars. Fingerprints would be taken as part of the booking process and those folks would be locked into jail cells as police work through their investigations. It might take a day or more before those reports reach prosecutors.

Prosecutors would then weigh the facts and evidence in considering how those actions meet the state's legal definition of self-de-

fense. Those finding themselves in that position would be thankful to be alive, but they'd still have plenty of stress in not knowing what's next. You could expect plenty of humiliation while sitting behind bars and feeling like a criminal.

With that foresight, a part the preparedness mindset extends beyond having the fortitude to use force when it's absolutely necessary. It should be everyone's goal to try to avoid threats. Whether it's a disaster in which a family bugs out or stays in place, the considerations are the same. Camouflage and hiding is the better part of valor. Amid serious and widespread unrest, hiding in a very literal sense would

be appropriate for family safety. In all cases, it's important to do everything reasonable to be as inconspicuous as possible.

Think about it in other terms. A woman walking through the Bronx late at night with a Rolex watch on one wrist and a big diamond bracelet on the other just painted a pretty big bull's eye on her own back. It's an exaggerated example, but it serves to illustrate the approach to life after a disaster. Aim to blend into the background. Avoid the fray. Those hunkered down at home shouldn't do anything that could draw attention to their property. People should aim to have a home that people would pass by without a second thought.

Those who have homes resembling Fort Knox can be certain the criminal element will take notice and want to investigate further. Those putting out the "No Trespassing" signs probably do so with all good intentions, but really, it's putting out an invitation. It's much the same consideration used in regard to concealed weapons.

It might be a matter of valuables. It might just be food, water and survival gear. Just like guns in an everyday situation, it's dangerous to let others know what's there or to even give them reason to think about it.

Even having a placard in the

There are many firearm training courses available. If you have the opportunity, it could be valuable to pursue some of these classes.

195

yard warning that trespassers would be shot is likely to do far more harm than good. If there's a big enough group gathered; the hoodlums might figure it's worth the risk of gunfire to determine what that household is so intent on protecting. They could surmise there's some pretty good stuff if someone is ready to pull a gun to protect it.

The home would likely provide your safest place should riot, looting or other crime become an issue in a disaster's wake. Within those plain, unassuming homes, the well prepared should have their firearms at the ready. A family, however, shouldn't let a gun or even several provide any false assurances of safety.

Guns and corresponding ammunition supplies might provide security should someone or even a few people break into any given home. In the midst of civil unrest, there's no reason to think a break-in would be limited to just a few. Should 20 people pour in through the door looking to haul off belongings, guns might only escalate the situation. Ammunition could fall short. It would stand to become an impossible and deadly situation if any of those criminals were also armed.

It's a matter of being smart. It's a matter of remembering that most possessions can be replaced. Lives are irreplaceable. Taking a stand might not be worth what any given person stands to lose. If it comes down to handing over a loaf of bread to a crook or pulling a firearm, it's probably the better decision to hand over the bread and not have to worry about standing trial after the smoke clears.

Firearms as preparedness tools do provide for plenty to think about. You could never know when and how a gun could become handy. Dangers beyond the criminal element might emerge from the havoc of a longer-term emergency situation.

On several occasions during my time in Iraq, we encountered dogs that reverted to wild instincts, gathered in packs and roamed the streets. We called them zombie dogs, and frankly, they were pretty scary. They certainly weren't the friendly dogs you'd want to approach with a biscuit or engage in a game of fetch.

It would be easy for some to dismiss that as a phenomenon of a war-torn, overseas country in chaos, but the possibility is just as real here at home. There have been a number of reports of vicious, feral dogs in the United States. That phenomenon had recently been subject of reports from economically battered Detroit and was attributed to people abandoning their animals. It isn't beyond reason to think it's a risk that people

Those storing guns and ammo have just two concepts to keep in mind: keep them cool and keep them dry.

Ammunition exposed to moisture would lend to corrosion that could potentially impact your ability to fire. The brass would turn green. It would corrode faster than steel. For the hunter, a damaged round could mean the rabbit — that night's dinner — is able to get away. For those carrying firearms for personal protection, a bad round could mean becoming a victim.

The ammo boxes built for military use are great options for long-term storage. They're readily available. They're air-tight and easy to carry. Put a desiccant in the box along with the rounds for further protection against humidity. Those who have vacuum sealers could take a great deal of ease in their long-term ammo storage by bagging it up and shrinking down. The sealers remove the air and take out all the humidity with it. The rounds would be just as good and ready to go when it's finally time to slice open the package.

Corrosion is just as much an issue for guns as it is for ammo. A gun owner should keep all of his firearms oiled. Those with firearms they don't intend to shoot for some time might apply some cosmoline to prevent corrosion. You should always keep dryers inside of the gun safe.

Those who live in particularly humid environments would want to pay close attention. You might keep a dehumidifier in the room in addition to the desiccants stored in with the guns.

Those who fail to take care of their firearms and ammunition risk a situation in which those tools might fail to take care of them. It's a matter of making sure there's a "boom" when it absolutely needs to be there.

Keeping stored guns and ammunition away from moisture is the only way to assure their future utility.

could encounter during any given rebuilding period should a disaster lead people to let their animals fend for themselves.

One of the overriding goals of preparedness is to have the tools needed to overcome whatever our challenges might be. Firearms fit into that picture. It isn't solely a matter of disaster. Anyone could be targeted for robbery tomorrow.

The criminal element is a very real concern in the wake of any devastation, whether large or small. It isn't always the violent mob. More often, it's the white-collar crimes. Fraud artists often come out in force whether by making telephone calls or heading door-to-door with elaborate stories and false services in effort to grab some cash or secure even more valuable credit card numbers. Violence, meanwhile, isn't always a matter of widespread trouble. Individuals might act on single moments of opportunity and draw their guns or knives. It would put your readiness to the test.

Looting and criminal activity was the reason I was hired to work in the aftermath of Hurricane

Katrina. I provided security for those working on the power grid. Members of our organization had a number of security roles in protecting key assets that could've been big targets for the criminal element.

Some, for instance, assisted in moving the money locked away in shuttered Gulf Coast casinos. Some businesses called on security to assure they could haul off all of their expensive and vital computer equipment without difficulty. Others accompanied engineers who moved from community to community to assess what was needed to bring electricity back to the region as a whole.

I witnessed a number of troublesome things during my time in post-Katrina New Orleans, but one thing I didn't see with my own eyes was the crime and disorder that led to my hire in the first place. Our show of force probably goes to explain that. The bad guys, I'm sure, knew better when it came to their own safety and took their activities outside of the sights of a fully-armed security unit. It provides something to consider. The record clearly shows that plenty of criminal activity happened beyond my view down in Louisiana. Be prepared. Most families don't have the luxury of hiring well-armed security teams to ensure their wellbeing.

Crime can have a big impact on a community after a disaster. After Hurricane Katrina, National Guard units and private security operations were needed to secure order in New Orleans.

8

PRACTICE MAKES PERFECT

Departments
conduct exercises to
simulate all types of
rescue situations.

Breaking down potential problems and gathering the right provisions mark the first big steps toward achieving readiness. Learning new skills along the way only makes your plans stronger. All of that work in itself, however, doesn't offer families much for guarantees.

The best laid blueprints for any

endeavor often fail to bring successful outcomes if they aren't scrutinized and worked through from beginning to end. It might be the efforts devised by the family preparing for a disaster aftermath. It could just as well be the high school football coach drawing up his plays for the big Friday night game. Plans can only flourish if they're followed up with sufficient practice.

Preparedness requires tools and abilities, but it's better defined by the diligent attitude that reminds us that even the strongest plans leave room for improvement. You might hold some family exercises to get a sense of how things would come together after disaster and to assure everyone in the family is on the same page. The diligent planner always keeps the mental wheels spinning, thinking through the next steps.

Those working toward preparedness should recognize the full extent of their capabilities at any given point in an effort to determine how to reach the next rung on the ladder. For instance, you would want to learn for certain just how much the family could power from the generator. It would make sense to figure out how much gas it burns in doing so.

Some might read the manual and generalize before it's finally time to put it to work. The most dedicated would flip off the breakers and check it out themselves. Putting the generator to work would offer a better sense of what you could and should use and what else in addition to electricity could help the family maximize its comfort when it's needed.

A weekend of eating from the emergency food locker might offer a clearer picture of how the family's comfort would hold up through an extended period. There are numbers of examples. All of that advance work allows you to fine-tune your readiness efforts.

It's important to have the right gear, but it doesn't mean as much if it isn't being used. You couldn't know for sure whether any given solution is workable until putting it to work. You couldn't assume your gear is reliable if it's sitting on the shelf with the price tag still attached. The night after the tornado is the wrong time to finally learn the unused tent that's gathered dust on its sealed box came with a tear or some broken poles.

Preparedness is more than a process of gathering. That's where practice becomes so important. Disaster situations are inherently taxing and by their very natures are bound to spring some surprises. You can't guess what's coming, but you can work toward having the flexibility needed to manage through the unexpected should a

disaster occur.

The rule of threes sets forth a pretty simple structure to get you started on planning. As such, preppers rarely have trouble identifying the right contingencies to account for the major issues most likely to develop from the risks in their regions. The trickier work always comes in determining and untangling many of the less obvious potential problems hiding in the fine print. Those smaller points tend to reveal themselves through practice.

Honing your readiness skills is really no different than the regular work of those placed in dangerous situations by virtue of their careers. Members of the U.S. military couldn't possibly go about their duties in war zones without the knowledge, skills and instincts they've gained through regular training exercises. Police departments regularly hold simulation exercises on a variety of potential emergencies, and often operations that rarely come to fruition. Departments will routinely hold exercises to prepare for hostage situations or the chance they'd have to deal with active shooters and mass casualties.

Firefighters routinely practice to build experiences they can rely

Firefighters go through practice exercises to help build experiences that they can rely on in real-life high-danger situations.

203

upon in high-danger situations. They'll conduct exercises to prepare for basement fires that have caused a significant number of fatalities through the years. Departments will conduct exercises that simulate response to high-rise blazes or aerial rescues. A number of fire departments have rappelling towers outside of their stations for training purposes. Few departments let a home or building set for demolition go to waste. They'll ignite those structures and use them for practice before crews bring in the heavy equipment to clear off the property.

Those examples aren't to say families need frequently intense, dedicated practice to meet their planning objectives. Rather, they point out that you can never underestimate the value of having some basis of experience to rely upon — even the simulated — when thrust into a stressful scenario. Families, like those professionals, should have enough background to provide an advantage when trouble comes knocking.

A prepper shouldn't get too comfortable. The family that went out, assembled a fully stocked shelter and declared the mission accomplished isn't necessarily going to be the best prepared when the big storm finally tears apart the neighborhood. The family of lesser means down the street that has a smaller cache of supplies packed away might well find itself in the better position if they kept up on planning, worked through their scenarios and are adept at solving problems.

Prepping isn't a project but rather a way of living that doesn't have an end point to work toward. There's no stage at which you could put your supplies behind a closed door in the basement and clear all those efforts from your mind until an event requires their use. Anyone could become stifled amid an emergency without some ability to adjust when and where needed. Those skills tend to grow with continual efforts and reassessment.

You could define practice to include all of the things — big or small — that build upon skill and knowledge and hone your abilities to react quickly. Practicing for recovery might mean gathering the family for deep, problem-solving discussions around the dining room table. It isn't always a time-consuming endeavor. It doesn't have to mean penciling time into the schedule book to pore over supply lists. Full weekend simulations would benefit a family from time to time. Practice, however, also entails simpler, daily engagement. Practice could be as simple as a few thoughts when spare moments allow.

Reading through books, blog posts or articles written by other

preppers could serve as practice, particularly if they offer ideas that hadn't previously come to mind. An afternoon splitting wood for the stove could fall into the category of practice. It might be a task needed to provide warmth to the home for the next few weeks ahead, but it's also a job that keeps your body and skills sharp should that job become a survival necessity.

Settling onto the couch with a puzzle in the evening could be considered part of your practice regimen. There's a lot of value in doing puzzles, whether it's word searches, crossword puzzles or Sudoku puzzles. The mind is the most important tool for survival and recovery, and you stand to gain by any means used to keep it sharp. Puzzles strengthen problem-solving.

Get the entire family involved and have some fun with the process along the way. Preparation is a way of life that should instill comfort

Police officers practice for emergency situations. You should too. Never underestimate the value of having some basis of experience to rely upon in a stressful situation.

and confidence rather than stress or undue worry of the dangerous possibilities. It's serious business, but for serious preppers, practice in some form is just part of daily life. Those who take on preparedness for peace of mind will have that much more in developing better familiarity with their efforts and greater confidence their planning stands to come through as devised when finally needed.

A family affair

Practice is quite important from the standpoint of assuring plans go far enough to meet a family's needs. It is just as vital, however, to ensure everyone in the household

The author's son tests a sleeping bag in negative 20-degree temperatures. You don't know if your equipment will work if you don't test it.

understands safety protocols and can confidently take on his or her roles should plans move into action. Unless you are living alone, preparation and practicing for a recovery will only fully serve its purpose if every member of the family is an active participant. Preparing shouldn't be construed as a concern solely for the adults in the household, because everyone would have a stake in getting through the aftermath of any disaster.

Some might question whether or how much younger children stand to gain from participation in the family's preparedness efforts. They too, though, should have a basis of understanding and some safety skills, even if limited and tailored to meet their maturity levels and abilities. A disaster, after all, isn't going to stop short and spare a home because there are scared children clinging to Mom and Dad inside. Mother Nature is a lot of things, but compassionate isn't one of them.

It's wise to think about how you would discuss preparedness when including younger children in the conversation. It'll take some sensitivity and a key understanding of how your children think and operate. It's nonetheless important they too have the mindset and abilities to not only make it through but also contribute to the family's recovery.

You certainly wouldn't want to scare the kids or create any undue concerns. If it's handled in sensitive fashion, the children will gain some knowledge, know-how and confidence. Moms and dads stand to gain some comfort in knowing the young ones have some degree of safety training. Overall, it stands to make the family's planning more complete.

When sitting around the kitchen table and walking through plans, the kids might very well come up with problems or solutions the adults didn't consider. They carry viewpoints unique to their age and experiences that could make any family's plan that much stronger. As parents, take the proper time, exercise patience and use the positions of love and trust to assure the children that danger isn't imminent. The kids should be led to understand the goal of preparing is to make sure everyone is as safe as possible all the time, even if by that slim chance something troubling comes to pass.

Every child should know the safe places to which they should retreat should dangers come to bear. Families in areas at risk of tornadoes should walk their children through all the important safety tips that apply to whether they're at home or out and about. Every kid should know where to go without a second thought after the sirens begin to sound.

The same would hold true for those at reasonable risks for earthquakes. Everyone should know the safest place to be wherever they might be. Families might establish meeting places, whether it's outside the nearby school or some other close-to-home landmark, should disaster happen when everyone is out and going about their days.

Practice in general should account for immediate-term safety considerations and offer a sense of what the family might experience in the days or even weeks to follow a destructive event. Troubles aren't over when people can finally dust off and recognize they weren't hurt. There are a number of ways in which families can run through their prep efforts, learn some important lessons and get a little enjoyment and bonding time along the way.

Plenty of potential dangers provide due reason to think ahead and teach our kids. Fire drills stand as one practice effort that's already common in some fashion to many families. Fire departments have done a good job in their educational roles in spreading the message of danger and reminding households of the importance of having a plan.

We'd run through drills on a somewhat regular basis when my kids were growing

If you have stored MREs, try some so you'll know how to heat them when you need the food to survive.

up. It's smart for anyone when considering the statistics. Firefighters were called to 370,000 house fires in 2011, according to the National Fire Protection Association. More than 2,500 died that year as result of residential fires, and it's fair to say it could've been a far lesser number had more been prepared.

We took that risk pretty seriously. As such, we took the time to make sure the kids had more than a simple knowledge of their responsibilities in the event of a house fire. We made sure they were able to respond to that emergency from positions of strength, confidence and habit.

The idea of a fire drill means different things to different people. The drills in the Nowka household weren't the carefree, walkthrough type of exercises that most children often encounter at school. I'd make for some pretty decent simulations of the real thing.

In the middle of the night, I'd occasionally roll out of bed, head over and press the button to sound the smoke detector. The kids would wake up, get on the move and I'd assess how well they responded. I'd keep an eye on how quickly they'd move and just how well they followed the established escape plans. We'd occasionally make it a full-scale exercise, roll out the window ladders and have the kids climb down. Those drills were always kind of exciting for the young ones.

Families should recognize the importance of changing things up to assure the drills don't become a simple matter of routine. Surprise strengthens practice. It's certainly important for every child to know escape routes and family meeting points, though kids learn more with an element of realism. House fires, like any emergency, are bound to carry the element of surprise.

In an effort to account for realism, I'd try to bring in one critical factor that's often missing from family simulation exercises. Those escaping from a real house fire would do so carrying varying degrees of stress. You can't overlook the significance of stress as a roadblock to safety.

Yelling is a common means used in many types of simulations to raise the stress levels of participants. A simulation's value only grows along with its ability to faithfully recreate what a person would go through and feel. People often fail to properly think through their situations and as result make poor, potentially dangerous decisions when experiencing anxiety, fear and pressure.

During our fire drills, I'd raise my voice and do some barking at the kids to get their stress to climb a bit while going through the exercise. When complete, I'd just as quickly gather them up and make sure they understood that the yelling wasn't out of anger. They came to know it was part of the process of making sure they had the mindsets and wherewithal to quickly, calmly and efficiently get to safety should the smoke alarm sound. I gained confidence. They were as ready as they could be for the serious potential of the alarm sounding without their father pushing on the button.

House fires are probably the most planned for household emergencies, and for good reason. It's a common and dangerous threat to which no one is immune. Those who are developing preparedness plans would just as quickly recognize those same characteristics apply well to several, potential threats. Those extending their family's planning to the greater list of dangers might consider other drills that would also provide opportunities to assess response and build skills.

Families are more likely to experience lengthy power outages than they are house fires. A family that's preparing would gain some good insight on their needs during a power outage by flipping off the main breaker and spending a full 24-hour period without electricity. I'd suggest getting permission from the spouse before springing a simulation on the family. It's yet another drill in which the family could extend its value through the element of surprise. You might excuse yourself and knock out the power during dinner or step away right before the family settles in for some television at dusk.

The idea is to hit the breaker without the kids having a chance to develop expectations and think through their responses in advance. It's bound to annoy the teenagers. You might experience pushback when the youngsters realize they're going to be without the television program they enjoy. For the younger kids, it might be an adventure of sorts. Everyone stands to get some good benefit.

The adults might test the kids from the get-go. Find out whether they know where to find the flashlights and other supplies that'll bring some immediate comfort in the early moments after the home goes black. Ignite the lanterns and talk about what the family might do in the morning in lieu of typical Saturday morning pancake breakfast. Encourage the kids to find some

You should practice starting a fire. It will make the task easier when you need heat as soon as possible.

fun that doesn't require an electrical socket, and hold hope it takes to their memories.

The exercise provides some good opportunities for the adults of the household. Some might determine a few more Aladdin lamps would make life a great deal easier. The grown-ups, too, stand to gain in finding out their comfort zones and determining their best bets for a little entertainment to pass the time. During the exercise, the family might prepare meals and grab snacks from the supply stored away for emergency use. Take stock of what the family reached for and went through before the kids cry "uncle" and Mom and Dad restore the power.

An electricity-free day every now and again might serve a practical purpose for some families. Those who purchase and store MREs as part of their preparedness plan will have to cycle through a portion every year given they

Cooking over an open flame is much different than cooking over a controlled temperature. Practice so you know what to expect.

typically have shelf lives of five years or less. Having some practice days throughout the year might offer some opportunity to crack open those cases getting closer to their expiration dates. It also serves to make simulations that are much closer to what the family could expect in a genuine recovery period.

Practicing with your preparations could become part of the summer vacation plans for some families. Those who are avid campers might consider leaving the trailer behind for one weekend during the summer and heading off to a primitive site in lieu of the high-amenity campground with the heated pool and electrical and plumbing hookups. Some families might enjoy the challenge. Some might not. They'd all stand to learn a few things from trying to live for three days on the contents of their go-bags.

A well-prepared family will have a bag assembled for every member. They're made to meet the needs of three days. Putting the bag to work outside of a survival situation in a controlled environment would safely allow you to assess just how well it would perform when it becomes necessary. The family that's woefully unprepared could get back into the car, enjoy the remainder of the weekend elsewhere and promptly get back to the drawing board come Monday. A real-life survival test wouldn't carry that same luxury.

A well-assembled bag will be fairly lightweight and provide for food, water and shelter through the course of those 72 hours. If put together right, it should allow a person to get through the elements with some degree of comfort. A good bag wouldn't leave any fear of falling on the wrong side of the rule of threes.

A three-day, go-bag camping trip might be a bit much for some members of the family. From a preparedness standpoint, it's important to figure out how well that assembly of gear would perform when it isn't a matter of recreation. You can't know whether it's sufficient until you put it through three days of work. They're a priority of preparedness, recognizing they're assembled for situations in which people might not otherwise survive without.

Pay attention during the weekend to how the family is managing. Is the MRE, or whatever is packed away for food needs, sufficient to deliver some degree of comfort? Are the kids dealing with some hunger issues? Is the family staying warm enough at night?

Merely arranging the trip would likely lead many to notice a few holes in their equipment lists. You might make plans and then come to realize you'll be sleeping outside and never got around to buying that tarp. The mind is often able to take better note of the details and recognize what was glossed over when it's finally time to put the preps to use.

The go-bag trip might not fall within the ideas of rest and relaxation that many look forward to during their summer vacation time. I wouldn't suggest it's an easy trip. From the standpoint of family peace, it might be a good idea to reserve a room at a nice hotel with a swimming pool to relax in at the end of those three days. No degree of discomfort could take from the value of the exercise toward having a better understanding of your readiness.

Different environments bring different dangers, and therefore some families might conduct drills that others wouldn't. Those living near wooded areas amid wildfire risks might conduct drills to determine how quickly they can get through their evacuation checklists, load up and get in the vehicle. They would enhance their safety and there's an opportunity to add an element of fun. Families might run a stopwatch during the exercise and see whether they can improve upon their times from one drill to the next. Most people enjoy a little competition.

Families that live in areas at high risk of tornadoes would certainly want to have some practice under their belts to rely upon

should an emergency eventually strike. Drills might be as simple as assessing how quickly the family can gather the pets and get to the safest area of the house. Occasionally, families might extend that practice and simulate how they'd respond to the aftermath of a destructive storm.

Those at the highest risk of tornadoes should have an extensive cache of gear to rely on should a storm level the home. The family would benefit from pulling the tools and supplies out the storage and setting up camp in the backyard for the weekend. Rely on MREs and other items packed away for emergency food needs. Cook outdoors if that's part of the plan. Pay attention to the little things. What's working? What's lacking? What's OK? What could be a little bit better?

Your takeaway from the weekend might be as simple as recognizing the sleeping bags that seemed like a good deal a few years back are too thin and far too uncomfortable for long-term use. You might find a leak in the tent and recognize it's time for a new and more durable model. Those living through a real-life emergency no longer have time to adjust if the cache of supplies isn't meeting needs.

Thinking ahead

Practice isn't always so time-

If you're new to cooking over an open fire, start with a meal that is hard to screw up and enjoyable.

A hardy skillet of potatoes is a perfect dish to cook over a fire.

consuming as a vacation or a weekend of power-free living from the house or backyard. One of the most meaningful forms of practice is a few moments of daily, mental exercise. Plans grow richer, deeper and more specific when preppers ask themselves, "what if?" and follow through the problem solving process one step at a time. In answering that question, those preparing will likely stumble across risks not previously considered. You might come up with new and better ways to address potential problems that have long been on the radar screen. Part of the idea is getting your mind in the habit of quickly assessing any situation from the standpoint of safety.

Preparing is all about anticipation. Often, knowledge and understanding gives you the ability to avoid dangers before they come to bear. In one instance, my adherence to preparation from the position of forethought might just have saved my life and those of two others.

A few decades back, I was hired to move an antique, 53-foot wooden boat down Lake Michigan and onward to the Tennessee River. Those of us onboard would've really been in some serious trouble if it hadn't been for a twinge of discomfort and an appropriate contingency plan. The boat was in pretty good shape for its age, but it hadn't been in the water for 20 years. That sparked some real concerns. All of my second guessing was matched by a certain degree of impatience held by the owners. They wanted to move. We agreed we wouldn't go until we had the right calm, clear, bluebird day to embark. I simply didn't feel comfortable with risking a bumpy ride.

Their pressure eventually wore on me. We split the difference and set out on a fairly calm day, but one that wasn't quite the level of calm I had in mind. I listened to my discomfort and prepared for the worst. I hauled in a generator, two different pumps, a selection of tools and one of those big-bag cellphones that was the only option at the time.

We started out among one-foot waves. Everything went well early on. We traveled beneath the Mackinac Bridge, which spans upper and lower Michigan. We were about four miles into the straits when the winds picked up and put three footers in our path. Waves of that size wouldn't normally be a big deal for that large of a boat, but that's where the story really begins. It started leaking like a sieve.

Water started rising. Wires shorted out. One of the boat's two engines died. The instruments weren't operating. We didn't have a radio. I called out for one of the owners to steer to the left of a lighthouse in the near distance.

In the meantime, I started up a generator, got a pump going and used the phone to inform the Coast Guard of our situation. I planned to run aground at the lighthouse, where we could wait for rescue. I was told it would take the Coast Guard 20 minutes to get a helicopter in the air.

I called back every five minutes to offer a status report. The water kept on rising and it wasn't easy to keep my calm. Waters reached the top of the oil pans and put the remaining engine at risk of cutting out. It was a long 15 minutes, but by my third call to the station, I could finally let go a sigh of relief. I noticed the pumps were making headway, and informed the Coast Guard we'd be able to make it six more miles to Beaver Island. Waves topped five feet by the time we reached the harbor.

If I hadn't planned ahead, we wouldn't have made it as far as

(top) The Worst-Case Scenario card game can help families consider their options in potential survival situations before they occur.

(above) Games like Chess help you strategize and keep your mind sharp.

Forethought is truly what saved the day. It provides a good example of the importance of asking, "what if?" My answer to that question was the pumps, generator and tools necessary to keep the boat afloat and deliver those aboard to safety. To be honest, a better answer to that mental question when thinking back to all of my early misgivings would've been to hold my ground despite the pressure of the owners. I should have kept that boat at shore until the weather finally met my level of comfort. Fortunately, the second best answer was still sufficient for a positive outcome.

Those adept at planning will make brief, pro-active assessments in a variety of situations. As a matter of habit, you should make sure to have your go-bag in the backseat of the car before embarking. My first thought when walking into a public place, for instance, is to identify two different ways out.

"What if?" is the simplest of questions, though it best defines why families take on preparedness efforts. A few minutes of mental exercise when time allows strengthens the diligent mindset. There's real value in working through all of the many things that could plausibly put the family at risk. When it comes down to it, there's an extensive list of potentially dangerous scenarios that fall within the realm of possibilities for every last house-

that lighthouse. We would've been in the water with our life vests and a few hopes and prayers. As I worked on keeping the vessel afloat, the owners of the boat had been oblivious to the fact that we were experiencing a pretty serious emergency. You don't have to look too far to find some tragic stories of sunken boats on the Great Lakes.

The mind is the most important tool for survival and recovery. Anything you can do to keep it sharp is a positive.

After the danger passed, I told them of the initial plans to run aground where we would've been plucked up by a Coast Guard helicopter. The two who joined me on the boat chuckled earlier that day as I loaded up all of that gear. I wasn't in the mood for a last laugh after we finally came to shore. We wandered into the bar and had a drink.

hold across the country.

It's fair to say the active, dedicated prepper, wherever he might live, could cross zombies or space invaders off of his readiness checklist. Aside from those admittedly silly examples, many will come to find there isn't too much you could eliminate without second thought. The risks of civil unrest, terrorism or chemical disaster might be highly unlikely for many people depending on their locales, but very few anywhere could credibly declare those risks as impossibilities. Just how would the family respond?

Walking through your list of the plausible doesn't mean you'd have to overextend efforts to account for the slimmest of possibilities. The exercise isn't one to suggest those with fairly low risks of chemical disaster should head out and buy

sets of HAZMAT suits for every member of the family. Mental practice, however, is an important component of preparation, because it pushes you to fully work through all of your options and abilities. It tends to instill some humility that in turn lends further toward that necessary, vigilant attitude.

You come to learn you aren't a superhero. Those who recognize their vulnerabilities are able to get past any ego or undue comfort and honestly assess how well they're prepared. There's always room for improvement. A thought process that's deep enough to recognize risks of lower likelihood puts you in a far better position to

Preparedness practice is about more than just going through a checklist. Make the practice as much like the real disaster situation as possible.

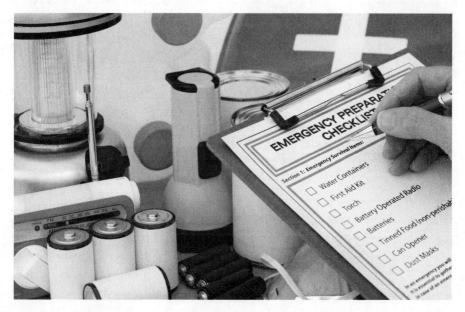

mitigate those of higher probability that appropriately draw the greater weight of planning.

Mental practice is just as valuable in the short-term and in the midst of potentially dangerous situations. It's a practice I've successfully put to use when called upon for underwater body recovery. Before and while in the water, I'd think about the possible things that could go wrong, and then match the dangers with possible solutions. I'd go from one possibility to the next with the mindset of keeping a few steps ahead of any difficulty that could threaten my safety as I went about my duty. I've actually found the process to be one that's served a dual purpose. The process kept my mind occupied and therefore off the stress and emotion that tend to make an already difficult task more troublesome for many divers.

As preppers progress naturally, they develop a drive to understand their strengths and weaknesses. Practice at that point simply happens. Those just getting started should pay close attention to where they've come, where they want to go and how well they're covered. Although it might sound obvious, an important part of your prepper's practice regimen is making sure you know how to use and feel

A well-assembled go-bag should be fairly lightweight and provide for food, water and shelter for 72 hours.

comfortable with each of the tools assembled for survival needs or disaster response.

As a matter of everyday living, keeping up with all of those tools might not be so easy of a task in recognizing the multi-faceted nature of any good plan. It wouldn't be so difficult for anyone to lose track of a few important tools along the way. What's out of sight is often out of mind.

Some people, for instance, might not have a regular need for their global positioning systems. It isn't difficult to imagine those folks forgetting about something even that crucial to a survival situation if it was purchased and packed in the go-bag among a greater assortment of gear. Think ahead. Upon making that purchase, it would make sense to plan a day in the woods or elsewhere and get accustomed to its operation. You should also figure out how to use the device in coordination with a map. Then you shouldn't let it sit long enough to forget the lessons picked up during those initial rounds of practice.

The GPS is just one example. It could be any tool. It isn't wise to pack away anything without first having some level of skill. A survival situation would become that much tougher should you find out you can't get through tree limbs with the small saw packed away in the go-bag. The disaster aftermath

One key piece of the preparation puzzle comes by any number of names but only one vital goal. When an emergency strikes, it's three days of survival that you could toss in the car or over your shoulder. They call it a go-bag or a bug-out bag. For others, it's a get-out-of-Dodge (or GOOD) bag. Some simply call it a 72-hour emergency kit. Regardless of name, it's crucial to have a decent pack at the ready.

The go-bag is a portable collection of gear designed to meet immediate survival needs. It's designed around the rule of threes with particular focus on shelter, water and food. The rule doesn't change. We can do three hours without shelter, three days without water and three weeks without food. Nonetheless, environments and individual considerations would vary.

Pre-assembled go-bags are readily available at many major stores and on the Internet, but ignore that temptation. Each individual is the only one who would understand his needs when all else fails.

Start with the bag itself. Grab something durable and waterproof. If nothing else,

Make sure to use a good quality pack for your go-bag.

make sure everything packed inside is sealed up and clear from the elements. From there, let the rule of threes lead the way.

Shelter is the immediate concern. Keep several fire-starting methods. I keep some WetFire cubes, a few lighters, some matches and a flint and magnesium starter in that portion of my bag. Have a poncho at hand. Keep a set of dry clothes inside. I also keep a silicone tarp and two-man tent.

Carry some water. Amounts might differ based on environment. In my water-rich region, I make sure to have a day's worth — a couple liters — at hand. Some would carry more. Those in drier locales should pack up the makings of a solar still. A water filtration pump is a great tool to assure you can replenish.

As for food, a high-calorie First Strike Pack military ration is a good bet. They're made for soldiers in combat situations.

In a survival situation, you could stretch its contents beyond 24 hours. A small fishing kit would provide another means of sustenance. Those carrying a firearm for protection could also hunt for small game.

Think about the variety of risks. Think about the climate. Pack in a good first-aid kit. Carry flashlights, a compass and a GPS unit. You should account for your specific individual needs. Some are caffeine dependent. Others have terrible, fall allergies. Families with pets or children should have the ability to provide care. Plan the bag accordingly. You might include a diversion or two. I pack a harmonica.

You should always have your bag at reach when traveling any significant distance from home. If survival situations were predictable, there would be no such thing as survival situations. A well-prepared bag would mean not only survival but also a certain degree of comfort for three days and even beyond if needed.

(below) In a survival situation, a First Strike Ration could last even longer than 24 hours.

(bottom) A small fishing kit can provide a means of sustenance.

is that much more stressful for the guy who's just pulling his water filtration pump out of the box and struggling through the instruction manual when clean water is an immediate need.

Survival situations also carry clear physical and mental challenges that could become easier through foresight and practice. The element of surprise in your family exercises extends beyond the value of recreating the moment that an emergency compromises safety. Whether it's the full family or the individual, a point of practice might focus on the ability to break from habit and routine. Many people settle into a fairly strict structure and run into stress when circumstances don't allow for the typical, relied upon schedule.

For many parents, life is often a matter of shipping the kids off to bed at the same time nightly and not a minute later. Many families have dinner on the table at the same time every evening. While working through recovery, broken routines could prove more difficult for some people than the actual challenges of the disaster. Families might find some fun ways to inject some flexibility and spontaneity into their lives.

Sleep routines are tough habits to break. Developing the ability to bank needed sleep when time is available could be crucial in an emergency. It might be an ability you could gain through some practice when time and schedule allows. Mix it up. Change things. See what happens and try to adjust.

Sleep was a real issue with a number of people I worked with in Hurricane Katrina's aftermath. The initial plans had been to work eight hours, then take eight off and repeat. Given travel times and other unforeseen glitches, that plan didn't work so we adjusted to 12-hour shifts followed by 12 hours of off-time. Some of the men down there, based on their normal routines, were having difficulty getting any sleep at all, and it took a toll on them.

A survival situation might force you to completely re-adjust your sleeping schedule. On scorching summer days, survival might require taking cover under shelter and getting that shut-eye during the hot hours to allow you to take on the strenuous activities during the cooler night time. Conversely, you might find yourself alone and having to keep a fire going for warmth during survival situations. That might mean sleeping 45 minutes at a clip and then waking to get fresh logs on the blaze before dozing off for another short period.

Practice could take a variety of forms depending on your needs. The guy whose job requires 100 miles of travel every day who is nervous about any level of car maintenance might benefit from taking off a wheel or two and then refastening them. It's better to struggle with the task in the driveway with all the time in the world and slowly build confidence. The only other option is waiting and falling into panic as traffic buzzes by along the highway when a tire goes flat. Avid boaters who spend time on the Great Lakes or any large body of water better make sure they're prepared to spend a full 24 hours out on the water if something goes wrong.

The honest, first steps are to look at how you live and search for the question marks left in the plans. All would like to think they have everything necessary whether from mindset or in appropriate gear. Practice is the only reliable way to make sure.

Plans can and do go awry, whether they're set up for the everyday circumstance or developed for those potential, difficult, extraordinary situations. Many have learned the hard way that what looks good, specific and complete on paper are none of those things when problems finally move from the hypothetical to stress-inducing reality. You shouldn't hope for the best. You should put your plan to the test and make sure it's everything you figured it would be.

Get accustomed to the operation of tools you might need in a disaster situation before one strikes.

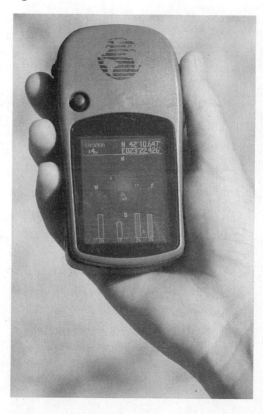

9

IN SHAPE TO SURVIVE

Working out with a partner might help keep you motivated.

One of the real, make-or-break aspects of preparation couldn't be packed away on a basement shelf or tucked inside of the go-bag. It's certainly important for preppers to consider their storage for the possibilities that lie ahead. Storage, however, wouldn't include that found on far too many waistlines in this day and age.

Health and fitness truly serve as the prepper's greatest assets.

It's absolutely critical to consider what you're putting into your body in terms of food and exercise if you are dedicated to preparedness. Getting through the aftermath of a disaster requires being in decent shape and in good overall health. There's no way around it. The best-laid, most detailed plans and supporting contingencies could tumble quickly if you lack strength or are battling weight issues or chronic health conditions.

It's not an easy truth to account for in an era where it's more common than not for people to wear a few extra pounds. Preparedness, however, isn't about glossing over the uncomfortable facts. Statistics clearly show those in decent physical shape have become the minority. Far too many, meanwhile, have fallen from average to the lower end of the scale and are managing their ways through poor health.

Those concerned about preparedness should hold real concern about their physical wellbeing and make appropriate changes to their lifestyles if necessary. It is just another part of preparation. It should be just as much a part of your plan as long-term food storage or assembling a well-stocked go-bag.

Should a crisis strike, those in its aftermath would need the ability to meet the significant physical challenges that are bound to stand in the way of a family's

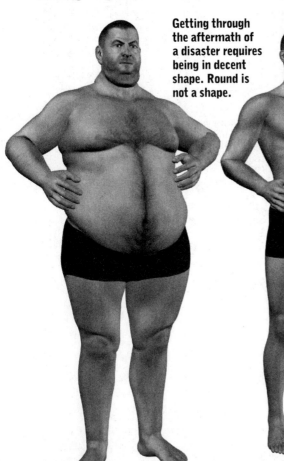

Getting through the aftermath of a disaster requires being in decent shape. Round is not a shape.

recovery. It would require some walking, and potentially for significant distances. It would require lifting. A crisis might require some climbing. Each of those tasks would certainly require some strength and a decent amount of endurance. Those who lack these attributes should concentrate on building up those "supplies" just as they would any others.

Fitness wasn't nearly as big of an issue even a generation ago. For most, it was just the normal, everyday state of being. It's yet one more example of how the modern convenience has done our society far more harm than good. Going back a few generations, most people didn't have to think about it. Fitness didn't require gym memberships. People didn't worry about squeezing in those 20 minutes of cardio per day. They got more than adequate daily exercise decades ago by simply heading off and accomplishing the day's work.

Some toiled out in the farm fields. Others took on the heavy lifting called for in our factories. They'd come home and accomplish yet more physical chores before finally heading off to bed. I wonder how many people back then could've even imagined what it would mean to live a "sedentary lifestyle."

Life is certainly different now. Technology kept on advancing and brought forth all sorts of cool, new tools aimed at bringing convenience to our lives. Any number of innovations certainly accomplished that mission, but some consequences came along for the ride. Today, the sedentary lifestyle is the unfortunate norm for a good number of Americans. It's more common now to earn a paycheck from the comfort of a desk chair while glued to a computer screen for eight hours or more each day. Many fail to pick up their activity levels after punching the clock at shift's end.

Televisions carry a couple hundred channels, and most folks have any number of must-watch programs penciled into their weekly schedules. For that matter, any number of tools — whether it's the dishwasher, the washers and dryers, the microwaves or even gas-powered lawn mowers — take care of, or at least lessen, the stress of so many household tasks that took far more time and effort decades ago. We're in a time like nothing before it. If people are unwilling to put forth some sweat and effort, modern living often doesn't require it. Many delight in that fact. I'm not so sure I'm one of them.

Exercise became a chore somewhere along the line. It's a bit frightening that so many of the youngest among us have never known anything but fast food diets and Nintendo leisure. Many children today are far more interested in pounding away at the buttons on their video games than hopping on bikes or engaging friends in games of tag or hide-and-seek. Many teenagers are hooked into their social media accounts and will spend entire nights chatting away at their computer desks.

Parents often fail to set a proper example. Many of us have laptops and tablets to keep the mind occupied. The couches are pretty comfortable. Frankly, it says a lot about society that a device was invented so that people no longer even have to step that long 8 to 10 feet away to turn the television channel.

Preppers might think and

respond differently. Preparing is a matter of taking steps beyond the commonplace in recognizing all the risks that could ever so quickly become reality. Amid crisis, typical convenience lifestyles would come back to bite the many who haven't bucked the system and kept themselves

Hiking is a great way to get active and get in shape.

in decent shape. Duty would call regardless of your aerobic capacity. Even the smaller-scale events as dictated by the rule of threes would likely create a real need for some real physical work.

Think about a hypothetical, severe thunderstorm packing high winds that rips through and topples the old oak tree in the backyard. You might lose power for a few hours. The electricity might continue to flow uninterrupted. The mess of branches might damage the fence.

You should stop and think about whether you have the strength and endurance to get that tree chopped up and out of the way in a timely fashion. After that wood is hauled off, you'd still have the task of making those fence repairs. Many today couldn't do it.

The general lack of physical activity in society at large is just one half of the damaging equation. We eat differently today and most often for the worse. Times seemingly changed overnight. For many families, the evening gathering at the dining room table is no more than a warm idea from a by-gone era known only from those black-and-white television shows. It was real life not all that long ago. Back then, the children might have fought some, but ultimately, they understood the expectation that they finish their vegetables if

Set goals for yourself on your way to getting healthier.

they wanted to have their desserts. They knew Mom and Dad weren't bluffing.

Society at large lives from the drive-through windows to a dangerous extent. Aside from those starchy, nutrient void, deep-fried potatoes that come in the combo meals, it isn't uncommon for some people to go for days on end without getting a single vegetable or fruit into their bodies. Stovetops and ovens better used for real foods get far less use than the reliable microwaves that make quick work of the heavily processed goods.

There's another danger at play. As time moved on, our portion sizes somehow grew larger and larger. It would be eye opening for many to look at recommended, healthy calorie intakes, then sit down and tabulate what they're actually putting into their bodies every day.

Most Americans are eating far too much. Far too few realize it. It's been a widespread and troublesome change. Those heading to the stores today to buy new sets of plates are typically getting sets of dishes that are quite larger than the pieces their mothers and grandmothers had stacked up in their cupboards. Compare one of their dinner plates to the comparable piece in the China cabinet. It might be eye-opening. It extends beyond the home. Many restaurants today choose to satisfy their customers with gigantic portions of poor foods rather than smaller, reasonable portions of fresh, local and healthy selections.

It would be simple to say people should be more responsible and keep watch on their portion sizes. It isn't so easy. Many don't know what a proper portion size looks like. There's another issue at play. It's simply nature for many people to keep on eating whether they're stuffed or not if there's still food sitting on those oversized plates. It's an area that takes some learning, thought and willpower.

The result of poor diets and sedentary lifestyles has rightly been called an epidemic. Our country has a problem with obesity like nothing before in our history. More than two thirds of American adults are overweight, while more than a third have sufficient weight issues to be considered obese, according to the Centers for Disease Control and Prevention. The statistics show just how quickly lifestyles have changed for the worse. In the early 1960s, only about 13 percent of American adults struggled with obesity issues.

Obesity, meanwhile, is an open door to any number of debilitating conditions. Some might come to struggle with heart disease. Obesity lends to an increased risk of stroke and type-two diabetes. It's been estimated that obesity is associated with 112,000 deaths every year. Many people lack the health and conditioning to guarantee full and fruitful living in even normal, everyday environments. Someone who can't manage well on the normal day would face a lightning-fast awakening amid the time of disaster's challenges.

Too few are getting their work in. As far as exercise goes, recent statistics have shown less than half of American adults meet the recommended guidelines for aerobic activity. Only one in five met the guidelines for aerobic activity and muscle-strengthening exercises.

Moving through a disaster, meanwhile, would mean a lot of real hard, exerting, "get your hands dirty," physical work. Depending on the nature of that disaster, it could mean a great deal of physical exertion through an extended period of time. The only solution is to get ready while you still can.

As a prepper, you would do well for your overall plan by honestly assessing your level of fitness without making excuses. Like all areas of preparedness, it starts with thinking about where you are at and where you really need to be. It's at that point the real work can begin.

There are plenty of people out there who couldn't walk even a mile or two without feeling a touch of strain and discomfort. Many would feel that certain tension in their muscles and find themselves huffing and puffing before finishing a mile. It should serve as a wake-up call.

Those in the worst of shape should take a moment to think about what they could possibly do if their very survival left no choice but go another 10 or 15 miles beyond the first mile marker. If it's frightening to some, it should be. They'd be in a helpless position after an emergency. It's a recognition that it's long past time to buckle down and get to work.

The out-of-shape folks who are otherwise dedicated to preparedness might think of it from another angle. Water filters are important tools that would lend a great deal toward survival should contamination become an issue. Generators are great tools that make life a great deal easier when the power goes down. There is no tool more important than the human body. It's the only one that truly matters. It's a tremendous piece of machinery, and it's critical that you assure it's running well when the ultimate test is calling.

There couldn't be a better time than the present for those struggling with fitness issues. Like many areas of preparedness, it's a component that would start slowly and gradually build to a level to which you could take some good comfort. The most important step is the first one. Start moving.

Anyone who's ever initiated a new exercise regimen knows that fitness isn't an overnight process. Those who are just getting started are bound to encounter some soreness along the way. The first few workouts might bring some misery during those next few mornings.

New fitness regimens start with a great deal of difficulty and become incrementally easier, day by day and week by week, as the body condition starts to improve. Most can feel the improvements step by step even if the mirror doesn't so quickly reflect them. It often makes the soreness that much easier to tolerate. The fit crowd likes to say that pain is what happens when weakness leaves the body. There's a good bit of truth there.

The importance of maintaining your fitness when considered from the place of survival or disaster goes beyond the immediate tasks. Troubles wouldn't disappear in a day. Fitness therefore also speaks to how you would handle the next day and those to follow. There's no leeway to take a day off to give the muscles a little more time for recovery after a good, long bout of strenuous activity. The chal-

Those with high blood pressure can often make significant strides in lowering their numbers simply by eating right, losing some pounds and returning to a healthy weight.

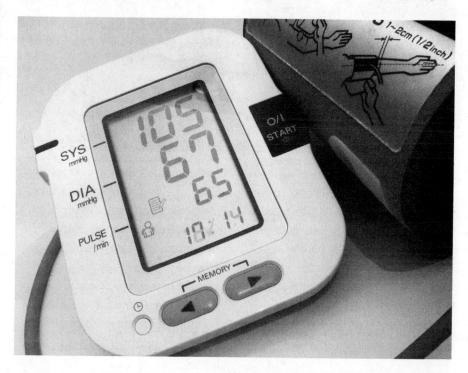

lenges aren't going to lie in wait until those tackling soreness are healed up and ready for the next round. Further, those who go too far beyond what their bodies are capable of handling run the risk of an injury that could present a dire turn of events.

Preppers are often as guilty as the next when it comes to ignoring fitness needs. There are certainly some out there who, while otherwise dedicated to the preparation lifestyle, fail to steer clear from the many unhealthy traps that tempt the majority. They're working against themselves. Those who exercise, eat well and have a solid degree of physical fitness would very likely be in a far better position to

the ability to make even a slow jog down the block. Without proper fitness, all of your other preparations in the end might provide a really nice collection of tools and supplies for someone else who kept his body in far better physical condition.

What is 'in shape?'

Those who watch television or peruse the magazines at the grocery store check-out lanes might get the discouraging sense that the world is made up of strong, muscular in-shape people on one side and "the rest of us" on the other. Fitness is another area where there's a happy middle ground. It's not an all-or-nothing proposition.

Everything that's accomplished toward health is a good step in the right direction. The washboard, six-pack abs on the men and women gracing the magazine covers aren't the blueprint of what's needed from the standpoint of preparedness. I'm sure many wives and husbands out there would be pleased with those results, but people in the midst of crisis would manage through with far less.

Those who are far less than world-class athletes can make their ways through survival situations and disaster aftermaths without worry if they are fit. Those scenarios would take appropriate strength but would not require becoming a muscle-bound specimen

When the author lifts weights, he tries to keep up his heart rate so the workout also helps with his cardiovascular health.

get through a disaster recovery.

Many might have that full array of gear that was carefully planned under the rule of threes to meet any number of situations. They're still in a losing position should they have high blood pressure, cholesterol issues and the need for a variety of medications. That position is made worse for those lacking

Both would often come to play at the same time. The go-bag provides an example. Mine has a diverse assortment of goods addressing shelter, water and food and weighs in at just more than 40 pounds.

For many folks, that doesn't sound like all that much, and honestly, it isn't a big deal to hoist it up and put over the shoulder. Then again, 40 pounds while standing in place carries a far different feeling than 40 pounds while on the move. That 40-pound bag feels far heavier after that first mile, and its stress on the body only increases with every step forward. A survival situation might require a 15-mile or longer walk with a fully loaded pack on the back.

The go-bag might not be the lone weightlifting you will encounter while out on the move. I remember having my 4-year-old son in tow a number of years back while taking the five-mile walk over Michigan's Mackinac Bridge. He did his best

who's able to compete for the Mr. Universe title. Having appropriate stamina to meet the tasks brought by a disaster wouldn't require the lifestyles of marathon runners or triathletes.

"In shape" isn't quite as easy to define as "out of shape." There's a very elementary way to illustrate what it means to have an appropriate level of fitness for survival or disaster recovery: "round" isn't among the shapes that'll cut the muster when trouble is calling. Those looking to make their way through tough times don't need chiseled bodies but should all the same strive to have lean frames and some muscle.

Those working through a survival situation or disaster recovery would come to realize efforts aren't a matter of strength on some occasions and endurance during others.

and I gave the youngster due credit, but by the time we were about a mile and a half into the walk, he didn't have another drop of energy to give.

I had to carry him the rest of the way. He made for quite the haul. If a crisis forces the family to move, the go-bag can't be left aside. If the family includes a young child or two, there's a good chance those youngsters will be carried for decent portions of the trek. It'll take some strength. It'll take some stamina.

Those new to preparedness would arrive at many different levels of fitness. Many do OK, but not great, when it comes to maintaining a healthy lifestyle. Many aren't dealing with obesity and the many other ailments that can branch from that unhealthy place. All the same, many could still stand to eat better on a more frequent basis and work at taking off a few pounds.

Building cardiovascular health is the primary task for those getting started. As a very basic yardstick, anyone in their 40s or 50s should still be able to walk five to 10 miles without much of a struggle. Those in that age group who aren't at that place should make a point to get moving whether it's a brisk walk or jog on a regular basis. You should always go a bit further than comfortable and allow the body to build.

The physical workload brought on by disaster situations isn't the only reason why health and fitness is so vital to getting through an aftermath. Healthy living in the here and now could prevent physical ailments down the road that would leave you vulnerable should access to medical care and medications be affected by a crisis situation.

Statistics pretty firmly show the relationship between health and the very abilities of people to make it through disaster situations. The elderly and sick, for instance, face the far greatest risks after disasters strike. The deaths caused by Hurricane Katrina very clearly show that fact. About 71 percent of deaths in Louisiana attributable to Hurricane Katrina involved victims 60 or older. About 47 percent of those were older than 75. Survival, regardless of anything else, requires some levels of physical ability and well-being.

Moving away from a "round" body type to that "in shape" state is not only important from the standpoint of preparedness but from the place of improving everyday quality of life. Those already struggling from ailments brought on by weight issues can often improve them with a renewed focus on healthy living. Those with high blood pressure, for instance, can often make significant strides in lowering their numbers simply by eating right, losing

A healthy lifestyle is essential to the survival mindset.

some pounds and returning to a healthy weight. For many, a change from the typical, All-American, fat and calorie-packed, fast-food diet to a reasonable, healthy, balanced and well-thought-out eating plan can lead to significant improvements in cholesterol levels.

Those who recognize preparedness as a practice in self-reliance should look at their required, daily prescription doses and ask themselves just how much they can truly rely on themselves. Medicine does some pretty amazing things.

In a survival situation, that might all go out the window.

Doctors are often reluctant to provide patients with any extra doses of medication to pack away for the event of an emergency. It's understandable when considering expiration dates. Medicines are regulated for a variety of reasons.

Preppers might occasionally find doctors who would oblige extra pack-away bottles of the prescription medications they depend upon after explaining their preparedness planning. Some doctors might offer up some samples that could be tucked away in the go-bag. All of that effort might still go for naught. If that's the best-case option, an extra 30 days' worth of medicines might not suffice depending on the nature of ailments and the severity of the disaster situation at hand.

It all comes back to thinking ahead. It's tough to imagine the helplessness of having a terrible heart condition and just a day's worth of doses left in the pill box. Many have diabetes and depend on daily insulin injections. Those with any serious ailments could find themselves in unenviable positions when all of the pharmacies in reasonable distance are dark, locked up and very likely emptied out.

Medicines are vital to many, and those with strict reliance could face imminent danger in a crisis. The wise decision for those who haven't reached the point of chronic ailments is to put forth some effort in the immediate term. Proper effort and attitude might well allow you to avoid a frightening set of circumstances later.

Getting in shape requires dedication, motivation and proper habits, but it's by no means an impossible journey. It takes work. It might take some willpower when that delicious and awfully unhealthy treat falls in sight. In many ways, it's just another exercise in common sense.

I'm neither a personal trainer, nor a dietitian. I wouldn't pretend to be either. Still, I think the biggest gains come at the very ground level and start with honesty. People generally know what they're doing wrong, but for some reason, they fail to correct their habits. It shouldn't take a trainer to say that a well-rounded dinner followed by a brisk, hour-long evening walk is far better than the up-sized, drive-through combo meal followed by a few television dramas. It doesn't take an expert opinion to know that an afternoon out on the canoe will do more for your health than hopping on the couch for a nap.

Help is out there for those who need it. Doctors and dietitians could offer some important advice as well as detailed diet plans for those attempting to lose a decent amount of weight or get certain health conditions in check. For a good number of people, I think there's still a lot of common sense value in an old-fashioned axiom about nutrition. Try to get several colors on the plate every day, and according to that rule, white — those starchy potatoes — isn't a countable color. It might be the yellow, green or red beans; that dark green spinach; or the burgundy beets.

There are a number of resources that are quickly available that offer solid information toward developing healthy and workable diet plans. The U.S. Department of Agriculture recently updated its dietary guidelines, which for a long time were represented by the food pyramid. Recommended food quantities vary for different people based on their varying daily caloric needs. Regardless of quantities, it provides a pretty good road map toward understanding what people should be eating.

The recommendations, which are separated by food groups, show the significant proportions of fruits and vegetables important in overall diets for the sake of health. For those who require 2,000 calories on a daily basis, the USDA recommends two cups of fruit and 2½ cups of vegetables. You would round out your meal plan with six ounces of grains, 5½ ounces of protein-carrying foods and three cups of dairy.

Relying on common sense and honesty about your poor personal habits provides a great start at getting an appropriate diet in place. You should recognize a meal with a small cut of lean meat aside several vegetables is a better choice than the frozen pizza. You should know the fresh produce in the bottom drawer of refrigerator will fuel the body in a better fashion than the large-sized TV dinner.

As for exercise, there are a variety of ways to build up endurance. You would need to be able to move and accomplish what could be critical tasks without getting winded in an emergency situation. I try to keep cardiovascular health in mind throughout my workouts and even when engaged in activities aimed at strength. If I'm lifting weights, just as when I'm on a treadmill or in the swimming pool, I keep a focus of keeping up that heart rate. If it's dipping, I bring up the exertion level to get that pulse back up to a decent pace.

Simply doing something would put a prepper in a far more active place than many. It's abundantly clear that most people aren't get-

ting nearly enough, or in some cases any, exercise. In 2008, an average of more than 25 percent of Americans reported having no leisure-time physical activity.

Healthy living requires a decent commitment. The CDC recommends the average person spend 150 minutes each week getting moderately intense aerobic activity. The agency also recommends the average person engage in muscle strengthening activities, working all the major muscle groups, at least twice a week.

CDC recommendations say increasing workout time or intensity increases health benefits or could give an extra stride or two toward losing weight. Workouts need not be for one extended period each day. A person will still get the same benefits from 10 minutes of aerobic activity at several points throughout the day as finishing a workout all at once.

There are plenty of options out there to get those minutes in. Gyms are great resources that provide any number of means for people to get that exercise. With that option, there's often good access to good

Cross county skiing is a great exercise activity for preppers.

advice from professionals on how to make the best and quickest strides to fitness goals.

Some aren't willing to spend the membership fees. Others can't imagine getting any enjoyment out of spending a monotonous hour on the treadmill. Those who aren't sold on the gym option can find any number of great means to get a workout. Some wouldn't cost more than the price of a decent pair of walking or running shoes.

Fitness advice and any number of workout plans are no further than a search of the Internet or a trip to the library. You might rely on the old standbys, whether its brisk walking or jogging combined with muscle conditioning exercises like pushups, sit-ups and crunches. Those who want to invest a little bit more into some workout tools, whether a few dumbbells or a pull-up bar, can do so at fairly inexpensive prices. We all know how many people start, then abandon their workout regimens. It's likely you could find any number of good items on the cheap by keeping an eye on the second-hand market.

I use the gym in the wintertime given the Northern climate isn't all that conducive to frequently getting outdoors for any extended physical activity. In the remaining three seasons, I try to get my exercise through outdoor activities. In many senses, it extends what my exercise has to offer. For purposes of preparedness, any number of outdoor activities offer a means to fitness and a way to get acclimated to what survival situations could present.

Exercising in the gym is a bit more controlled, and in that way, quite dissimilar to the experience of hauling off debris or other tasks more likely in a disaster aftermath. Lifting weights, whether with gloved hands or padded bars, would quite likely be less taxing than chopping and hauling off some wood. Walking on a treadmill or jogging on a smooth and even track is going to be far easier on the body than walking or jogging on the trail.

Trails are a great bet. They offer scenery but also give you shifts in elevation and all of the bumps and crevices that could lead to blisters and all types of soreness for those who aren't accustomed. It's a smart plan to get the body acclimated early to the rougher stuff that Mother Nature presents. It's one less thing that could trip up a prepper after disaster.

The hikers who tackle the Appalachian Trail provide a good example and further show what the extremely well-conditioned can accomplish. Its full length serves as a rite of passage for a small handful of people every year and extends nearly 2,200 miles from Maine to

BASIC WORKOUT EQUIPMENT FOR THE SURVIVALIST

The world is a gym. Anyone who wants to get started on a good workout regimen needs only three things and not one would cost a penny. The body and the environment provide all you would need from the physical angle. Discipline is always the deciding factor on whether you are ultimately successful.

The most important pieces of workout equipment for any survivalist are his own two feet. It helps to have a good pair of shoes. You might not have a gym membership, but you might have a nearby hill. That alone could be enough to get you from round to lean with the right effort. Walk up. Jog down. Repeat. When the workload becomes easier, you might jog both ways.

Chop wood. Work in the garden. Mow the lawn. Anything that takes some physical effort is contributing to your health. It's a matter of thinking about what the body needs, setting goals and putting in enough time and work to reach them.

It all comes back to discipline. Take a walk. Take a jog. You could make a great deal of headway on your health by picking up your go-bag and taking three or four laps around the block. Make it a habit. Do it nightly. It would account for strength and endurance.

There are many roads to fitness. Some people might want the big weight set and the expensive elliptical machine. Gym memberships do work well for many. The money spent might provide a good level of motivation. It isn't necessary.

Those who are willing to spend a little money on getting in shape might consider TRX straps. They're made of nylon webbing and give you the ability to build up strength off of your own weight. The exercise comes from resistance.

The nylon straps are an inexpensive option and they're versatile. You could take them anywhere. The prepper who checked into the less expensive hotel without that nice workout room could hook them to the door and accomplish all of the same. Crafty folks could make their own versions.

When push comes to shove, it really isn't a matter of equipment. The only real factor is your dedication toward getting fit and healthy. Machines can't do it. It's the willpower, habits and efforts of those standing upon them.

If you really want it — whether it's in a gym, on a hill or walking around the block — you will find your way to make a healthier life happen.

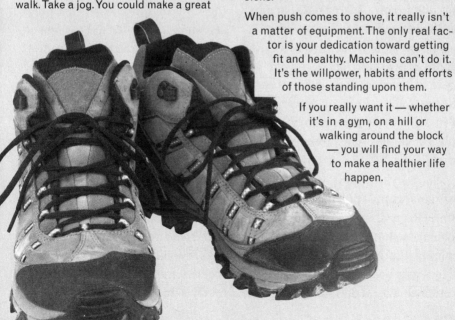

Georgia. Many, many people enjoy far shorter stretches. Whether it's the weekend 20- to 40-mile trek that's common for so many or the month-after-long-month endurance challenge that extends across much of the width of the United States, we can pull out some good ideas.

For many hikers, 20 miles or more each day is a pretty common goal. They'll have a light pack, not much unlike our go-bags, loaded up to meet basic needs along the trail. They'll stop halfway for lunch and a decent rest and continue on for the second half of the day's journey before setting up camp for the night. When the sun rises, they'll do it again. For many, it's weekend recreation. The well-conditioned few just keep on going and going.

With that model in mind, a good endurance test might be that nearby, public trail. Take a pack, head out for 20 miles one day and then sleep the night before heading back in the other direction. You could note how you feel and use that as a gauge to determine whether your fitness level is appropriate when placed against your preparedness plan.

The nature of your exercise isn't as important as putting in the time. Regardless of your workout plan, you should assess how your incremental growth compares to what your body would need to accomplish after a disaster. It might just provide some motivation to keep going.

Exercise is another area in which I try to live my preparations. I often try to get some of my exercise in means that add to my skill base for use in an emergency. I regularly chop and split wood. It provides a great workout, but I'm also practicing and know I'm firm in my techniques. Readying wood for a fire after a disaster wouldn't provide for any major challenge or frustrations because it's already part of how I live.

Swimming is another example. It's a tremendous cardiovascular workout. It's also a skill that people might need in a crisis situation.

Like anything else, workouts are less about work for those who actually enjoy the time spent on physical activity. Find some activities that are fun and get that pulse elevated. I, for instance, will get out on the lake with a rowboat from time to time. It's a strength exercise, it meets those cardio considerations and it also provides for a heck of a nice day.

Think about the possibilities out there. Though no two survival situations are the same, it's worth considering some of the scenarios that would require physical exertion. No one can go more than three days without water. Survival might require traveling some distance to find a source; then hauling several gallons to the camp where the family is waiting. You might have to hike a tremendous distance to the main road or nearest town with that heavy bag on your shoulders. Consider the strength, balance and coordination it could take to continue forward as well as climb up and over any obstacles along the path.

Healthy living and often the lack thereof interestingly shows that what people want and the effort they're willing to put forth to get there are two different things. In the greater sense, there isn't a person who wouldn't want to live to be 100 years or older. Very few are disciplined enough to treat their bodies in a fashion that might give them the chance to get there.

It further goes to show how health fits into your preparedness plan. Preppers live differently. The efforts taken in preparing are a matter of putting forth work now in hope of achieving the right outcome later. Health is really no different than any other part of the plan.

When it comes down to it, there's nothing to lose and everything to gain from moving into a healthy lifestyle. Those prepared in every which way but health might think of one tremendous disaster that's on the radar screen and easily avoidable. You should think about your body at age 60 after years of unhealthy habits. It might very

well qualify as disaster, and it's one many create for themselves. Those who get their bodies into better shape and maintain that conditioning might eventually consider it a disaster averted as they advance in their years.

Of course, there are the fortunate few who get through their time on this planet without having to experience some sort of hardship. No one should count on being among the lucky ones. You can't predict how natural disaster could affect your life, though living well provides the best bets against self-inflicted ones.

Getting into and maintaining a healthy lifestyle — keeping in shape — truly is the most common sense endeavor you could take along the path to preparedness. Those headed to the home improvement store to buy a generator do so with the hope they'll rarely have the circumstances that would allow them to collect on that investment. No one is hoping to live for any extended time in a tent.

Anyone would collect the benefits of healthy living every day. There's something to be said about simply feeling better. As an add-on, preppers have the comfort of knowing the most important piece of machinery in the cache — the human body — is well fueled, tuned up and ready to go should tough times come calling.

10

MEDICINE WITHOUT DOCTORS

A well-stocked first
aid bag is essential.
Knowing how to use
it is more important.

Readiness isn't an easy path, but it's certainly worth all of the effort that's needed to get there. One component in particular might be pretty tough for some people to consider. Medicine, it would seem, is probably the most notable area in the realm of preparation in which people of our era might shun the notion of self-reliance. It's all

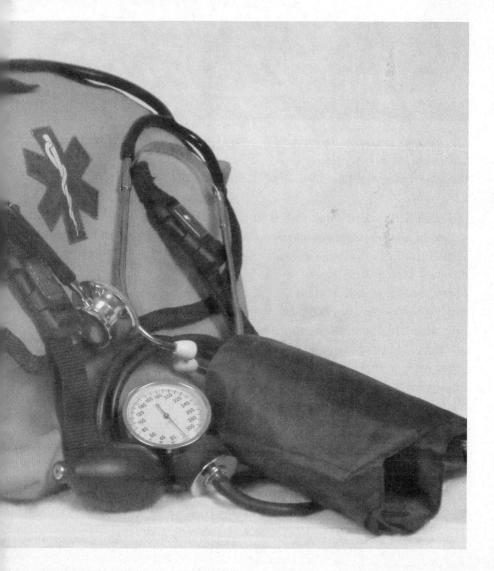

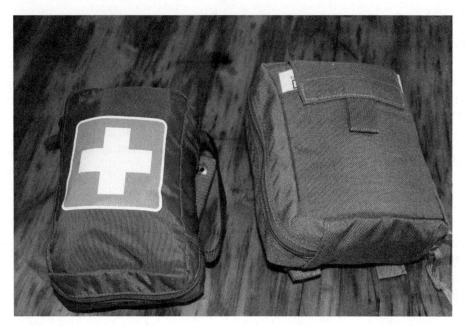

the same an important effort and one every bit as essential as any other part of a well-laid preparedness plan.

For some, it might come with a degree of apprehension. Modern medicine, after all, stands among our most tremendous assets. Members of the medical community represent society's best and brightest. They've underwent years of specialized education and training to achieve their credentials. Their work requires a steady hand, smarts, care and confidence. Often, there's little room for error.

Those who work in emergency response, meanwhile, make their livings in environments of high stress and higher stakes. They're ready to move at the very moment a call comes in. It's amazing to think of the balance and concentration that all of our medical professionals maintain as a matter of habit when people are in pain or lives are on the line.

The author carried these two first aid kits on him while in Afghanistan.

Injuries and illnesses are tough for many to think about. Taking responsibility for a person's wellbeing might carry some intimidation. It requires calm and nerve. It's easy to understand how the greater number of people out there might shudder at the thought of going it alone.

Preppers, however, understand just how quickly life could change for the worse. The best or most favorable option isn't always an available one. Everything we typically rely upon, including medical care, could disappear at a moment's notice. It's happened before and it will inevitably happen again.

You could stumble into a situation in which you're forced to provide your own care. You could become lost, endangered and have no chance of any aid beyond the provisions carried in your pack. A 911 call couldn't offer relief if you're in a desolate locale beyond the reach of cell phone reception. You'd be on your own should you trip, stumble and significantly gash your leg on a jagged rock. You'd have to reach for your first aid kit. It'd be important for you to know how to properly use the goods packed inside.

The community as a whole could find itself reeling after an act of nature. Someone who emerged from a tornado with a broken arm might have to wait several hours or even longer for professional care if the community's entire medical infrastructure is tied up and attending to those with life-threatening injuries. The situation would provide for less panic, pain and hardship if he or a loved one knew how to apply a splint that would suffice for the meantime.

Doctors would always be the most preferable option when illnesses and injuries go beyond the common and minor. As a matter of self-reliance, all people should have at least a minimal ability to offer their very best in terms of care should the time and need eventually call. The health and wellbeing of our family members and others we encounter — for that matter, our very own health — fit squarely within the most basic reasons for planning ahead.

The rule of threes isn't about what makes you comfortable. It's about surviving. People could very easily run into a position of having to survive without the aid and knowledge of doctors.

Too many fail to think about just how much disasters would strip away from a community. Obtaining a doctor's care or advice wouldn't be as simple as a phone call or trip to the nearby walk-in clinic. They'd have their hands full. Summoning help to an emergency scene might not always be as easy as dialing 911. Emergency dispatch systems might be knocked out. More likely, the entire ambulance fleet would be out in the community scrambling from injury to injury.

Any bit of knowledge is better than none at all. Even basic first aid skills could give you a real ability to bring calm to an otherwise frantic situation. At the very least, you could provide the injured with a better ability to wait for more substantial intervention. Having an understanding of illnesses and their causes would allow you to steer your family members away from some pretty significant dangers. Disasters often bring hazards at every turn.

Preppers wouldn't have to move past the basics. You wouldn't need to embark on the path toward a nursing or medical degree. Having a solid basis in preparedness wouldn't require you to achieve an emergency medical technician's license. A prepper wouldn't attempt a self-surgery. It isn't a matter of knowing it all. It's simply a matter of knowing enough.

Health is always a major con-

This was the Military Improved or Individual First Aid Kit — IFAK. It is really a trauma kit for major injuries.

cern after disaster. Prepping in general is an exercise in taking our wellbeing into our own hands. As a responsible and compassionate citizen, you might also have to take on the role of care provider for another if there's no one else available with better skills to handle the task.

Getting to that place requires some work in the everyday calm.

The health risks after a disaster could become substantial. People get hurt. People become sick. Damages left behind in the wake of storms, earthquakes or any other life-changing event would open all

kinds of new hazards that wouldn't exist on the typical day.

Greater risks of trauma would exist through all the rubble and debris scattered about. Illnesses have been known to settle on communities in the weeks and months beyond a disaster. The aftermath of some quite recent disasters illustrates the atypical risks those struggling might encounter after calm re-emerges.

Health workers after Hurricane Katrina noted outbreaks of some serious diarrheal illnesses within the mass shelters opened to accommodate evacuees. Testing conducted on those suffering revealed causes that included salmonella, cholera and noroviruses. Those illnesses were directly attributed to the aftermath of the hurricane.

Several others who made it through Katrina developed staph infections. Health workers diagnosed vibrio illnesses in several people after the hurricane. The bacteria caused five deaths. It's believed most of those who contracted the illness were infected through open wounds on their bodies when they traveled through contaminated floodwaters.

Medical workers in Missouri dealt with several patients carrying a rare fungal skin infection in the aftermath of the 2011 Joplin, Mo. tornado. The illnesses were thought to be caused by soil and vegetative

materials becoming imbedded in open wounds. At least three people died as a result.

New York City and its metropolitan area managed through a number of public health concerns after Superstorm Sandy pushed through in 2012. Concerns included mold and issues of sewage, oil and other contaminants that are typical

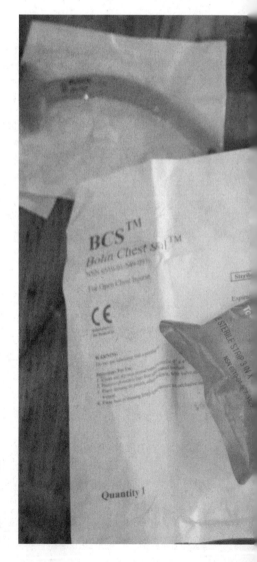

of any flood disaster. There were also fears of disease outbreaks from the drowning and decay of the city's urban rat population. Additionally, there were fears regarding the heartier rats that survived and were displaced from their subterranean homes to the surface by floodwaters.

Public health officials have raised generalized concerns that can affect the wellbeing of communities after disasters. Flooding, whether brought by hurricanes or otherwise, typically brings forth worries of the West Nile Virus. It's an illness carried by the mosquitos that

These are the contents of an IFAK. Soldiers carry these kits so the medics don't have to carry so much.

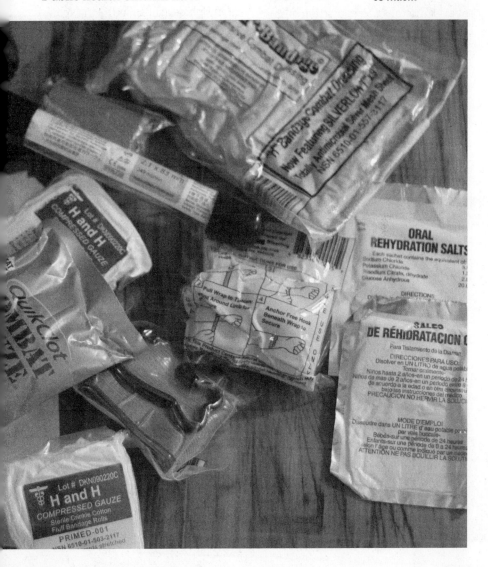

would obviously thrive amid wide spaces of stagnant water. The CDC cites a variety of health risks to consider after disaster ranging from tetanus and chickenpox to the water-borne Crypto and Giardia parasites.

The list goes to show that a community's overall health can take a pounding from disaster just as does everything else. Preparation from the standpoint of medicine means developing a strong respect for the increased chances of illness that accompany destructive episodes. Readiness recognizes that you can never be too careful. Prevention, as it's been said, is always the best medicine.

Someone who's prepared would also be quick to recognize a stark reality that settles in as storms pass: doctors, hospitals, ambulances, nurses, paramedics and all else that contributes to a community's health and wellbeing aren't immune from the devastation. Our medical infrastructure would face the same serious challenges as the overall community. That alone places those suffering from health problems at far greater risk than they'd experience on a typical sunny afternoon.

Recent history has shown the overwhelming trials endured by health systems in the wake of disaster. Any emergency means heavier

First aid kits are a vital piece of the prepper's overall cache.

workload for anyone making a career of serving the public. Often, disaster means our professionals have more work and far less capability to handle it. Hospitals might have a more important role than many buildings in our communities, but they're brick and mortar — and therefore susceptible to damage — like any others.

Several hospitals in and around New Orleans sustained significant flooding among other damages and were forced to close after Hurricane Katrina's 2005 wrath. Some of those facilities never reopened. The damage left by that storm impacted the general public's access to health care at various levels for years after the floodwaters receded.

Workers at St. John's Regional Medical Center in Joplin were left without a facility after the huge and destructive 2011 tornado tore through the structure. The tornado's impacts were also long felt. Medical crews resumed care from tents shortly after the storm. They later moved into trailers. In 2012, hospital operations moved into a pre-fabricated building as plans for a new community hospital continued to unfold.

Manhattan's NYU Langone Medical Center and Bellevue Hospital were shut down after Sandy in 2012. Both suffered power outages and neither were able to restore their power through generators.

The storm forced the evacuation of about 800 patients between the two facilities.

Crisis situations go beyond a matter of buildings. From a medical aspect, Joplin truly experienced a worst-case scenario as the massive storm tore through the city. St. John's took a direct hit from the tornado and sustained severe structural damage. Workers had to evacuate 183 patients after the storm passed. Six inside the hospital died.

When examined from a wider view, the devastation in Joplin provides a stark illustration of the stress and difficulty communities might face from the realm of public health in the early hours after disaster. Search and rescue operations began quickly after calm settled in. The region's second hospital, Freeman Health System, took on critical care patients from St. John's and picked up as much slack as it could in service to the greater community. It wasn't enough.

Each of Joplin's clinics and other healthcare facilities quickly reached capacity as the injured were located and ushered to safety. Medical personnel did their best with what they had. They set up triage locations throughout the city, including at the high school and even in store parking lots, to provide what treatment they could to those who were hurt, according to

FEMA. Those with medical expertise had to rely on some degree of creativity from those spots given a shortage of adequate medical supplies. It wasn't easy.

Americans are certainly blessed to have an overall emergency response system that can move quickly. It was shown in the tragedy of Joplin. There were nine ambulances in the field within the first 10 minutes. There were 21 ambulances and almost 70 EMS providers in the field within a half hour. Within the first hour, they transported about 350 patients. Within a week, members of the St. John's medical staff were able to provide treatment from a 60-bed mobile field hospital brought to the ravaged city, FEMA reports.

That region did the best it could under strikingly difficult circumstances. Its responders did amazingly well as they waited for the greater relief effort to build around them. It all the same goes to show how quickly our strongest community assets can fall vulnerable. It takes just a few minutes of time.

Preppers might take away yet one more lesson as it pertains to the urgency of planning needs. Collaborative efforts on a regional and even national scale are strong. Others would always come in from the outside to bolster any community's ability to manage an otherwise unfathomable situation. It might

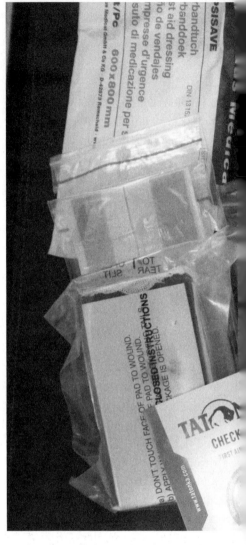

take hours. Calm and safety might take days. It provides little solace to those injured and in great pain at the very immediate moment.

The difficulties presented at the onset of disaster takes nothing away from the men and women who give their all when it's time for duty. Emergency response in the wake of disaster really boils

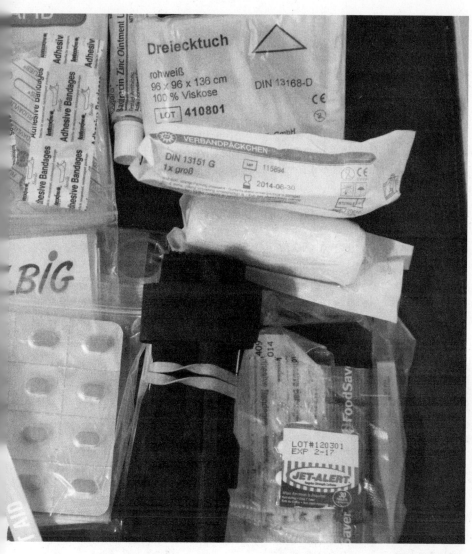

You can personalize your first aid kit to fit your needs. The author added caffeine pills, antibiotic ointment, antihistamine and a tourniquet to this kit.

down to simple arithmetic. On the typical day, emergency medical services can move at a moment's notice when one, two or even a few emergencies require efforts in several areas of a smaller city on a simultaneous basis. If that city has six ambulance crews, there simply wouldn't be any good way to promptly or adequately deal with

20 or more calls that reach 911 dispatchers just moments after the disaster gives way to calm. There's no reasonable way around it.

I've long held a deep appreciation for the emergency workers who manage with little before outside aid gives suffering communities some means to take control. I worked as a lieutenant at our local fire department in the early 1990s. We had a large and mostly rural coverage area. The unwieldy square mileage of our jurisdiction really got the best of us when several tornadoes touched down on one Saturday afternoon in September.

Our area fortunately made it through those storms without deaths or any serious injuries, but to say our department was spread thin doesn't begin to explain that work day. We were completely overwhelmed. Our department had 20 members out in five trucks and we were covering calls at every corner of our sizable service area.

By the end of the day, our crews worked through nearly 100 calls for service and half or more came in the earliest hours. We did the very best we could. It's tough to imagine that same situation had a number of those calls involved people who suffered serious injuries.

Disaster provides a heck of an endeavor for any agency of any type. It isn't a matter of the effort put forth by the men and women out in

Choose your path carefully. A turned ankle can become life threatening in a disaster situation.

the field. They're very assuredly giving their best. Fire departments, police departments and ambulance crews would inevitably be working in a situation where needs far outweigh the abilities to promptly meet them.

Medical teams would face much the same situation as our police officers, who often struggle to balance law enforcement duties with search and rescue and general public safety when widespread and scattered needs emerge after disaster. It's always a mess. Our full medical infrastructure — from the dispatcher taking the 911 call to the nurse delivering care at the hospital bed — would very likely struggle with far more patients than they're equipped to handle. Capabilities at the local level in any community from the smallest town to the sprawling metropolis are only designed to meet the needs of a typical day.

Prepping is a matter of reaching good solutions at the individual level before the problems that have been documented elsewhere finally strike home. It's a practice that's supported with the right gear, though it isn't defined by what's in the toolbox. It's a matter of attitude. Post-disaster safety and the potential need to treat injuries will require some effort and the right mindset. It would also require just a little bit of education.

All people, preppers or otherwise, should take the time to get their certification in cardiopulmonary resuscitation. CPR could provide the lone opportunity to save another's life if he or she is without a pulse and isn't breathing. It might be a heart attack. It could be a number of other causes. The courses take only a few hours and they offer the potential to save a person whose very life hinges on just a few critical minutes.

It's a skill that is just as important for the average day as it is for disaster. You should never assume that another would have the skills necessary to take on that critical life-saving task at a time of need. It comes back to self-reliance. It's a small amount of time that's incredibly well spent.

Everyone should take basic and advanced first aid courses. They'd give you the opportunity to handle potential trauma in the wake of disaster. First aid training, like CPR, also provides a good skill set for every day. Accidents happen. Health conditions put people at critical danger all the time. Those trained in first aid have the vital ability to start care in those all-important minutes before an ambulance arrives.

It's important to consider all of the good that could come from just a small amount of training. Having the ability to treat even a minor wound could provide the injured with calm and comfort until he or she is able to see a professional. That good would stretch yet further in having the ability to treat an injury during chaotic times when risks abound and there's no guarantee of any professional's speedy arrival. A prepper might offer the injured his very best chance.

Classes on first aid are widely available and regularly scheduled wherever you might live, whether through organizations such as the American Red Cross and the American Heart Association, community colleges or often at hospitals and fire departments. They're often hands-on courses and cover a variety of health topics from simple wounds to potentially life-threatening situations. Many first aid classes take only a day's time to complete.

Those enrolled learn how to handle bleeding. Lessons range all the way from the cleaning and dressing of a simple cut to proper use of a tourniquet that would halt significant bleeding after a potentially critical injury. The full range of those skills could become very important. It's easy to envision encountering wounds of varying gravity amid the wreckage both immediately after a disaster and as clean-up presses forward.

The courses would teach you how to handle minor bone breaks.

Courses address the treatment of burns and sprains. You would learn how to care for those experiencing seizures or suffering from heat- or cold-related emergencies.

It's valuable information that fits in well with the greater scope of your emergency planning. First aid isn't always a matter of life or death. Someone who can properly treat a minor issue — whether it's your own or that of a family member — is able to get right back to the bigger tasks at hand.

Some preppers out there place higher emphasis on the medical aspects of their plans than others. Some get through the courses designed for everyday folks and decide they'd be more comfortable with a more detailed base of knowledge. It all comes back to the level of preparedness you are seeking.

Some of those with deeper plans, for instance, took the time and effort to learn how to do stitches. You wouldn't have to go that far. That's particularly true for those preppers who have an adequate stash of supplies at hand. It comes back to flexibility and having a well-rounded knowledge that touches the many areas of life that stand to be impacted by disaster. In most cases, the super glue or duct tape in the workshop or kitchen drawer would suffice to close all but the most serious wounds sufficiently until you could reach a health professional.

Supplies do become important as it pertains to potential injuries. It's important to have a sufficiently stocked first aid kit at reach. First aid kits are a vital piece of the prepper's overall cache.

Every kit would include the basics, including a good supply of bandages, gauze pads and painkillers. Many would decide to pack in a tourniquet and do so with strong hopes they'd never encounter wounding so serious as to require its use. A good kit as it relates to disaster preparedness would include a decent supply of triple antibiotic cream for use on even the smallest nicks and cuts.

Never underestimate the value of duct tape. In most cases, it would help close all but the most serious wounds until you could reach a health professional.

Proper cleaning and dressing of wounds is important every day. It's more so during a survival situation or following disaster. You can't take chances. A prepper would recognize the quick and severe difficulties infection could pose and the complications it would bring to the overall efforts a disaster aftermath requires.

The knowledge offered through first aid courses and capabilities provided by kits give a prepper greater personal advantages when recognizing the foremost goal of preparedness is simply staying alive. Injury or illness could severely limit the chances of you making it through a survival situation. The rest of your preparations couldn't make up the difference.

Basic first aid courses are vital if for no reason more than gaining enough knowledge to recognize the causes of common illnesses and their early symptoms. Simple recognition could go a long way toward managing through disaster and back to safety. Being able to recognize a problem or potential hazard is really three quarters of the battle.

The fact that several of the deaths from 2012's Superstorm Sandy were caused by carbon monoxide poisoning speaks to the importance of proper knowledge. It speaks first to avoiding tremendous dangers such as the indoor use of generators. You could further wonder whether if some of those deaths might have been preventable had victims known enough to recognize something wasn't right and went to fresh air.

A proper understanding of health and the corresponding ability to account for the family's wellbeing draws from a variety of preparedness topics. It comes from recognizing the necessity of proper hydration and the significant dangers posed by consuming contaminated water. It's built from recognizing our bodies can't function when below or beyond their healthy normal temperatures.

Those who understand the early symptoms of dehydration, for instance, would then have the ability to shift gears and make water the top priority before the danger grows more significant. Those who recognized the earliest symptoms of hypothermia or hyperthermia might well have saved their own lifes. When a health risk provides a person only three hours to correct the problem, there isn't a single minute to spare.

Wellbeing after a disaster requires a sense of caution even

Basic first aid courses are vital for preppers. Being able to recognize a problem or potential hazard is invaluable in a disaster situation.

greater than what you might exercise on the common day. Those who get hurt during a recovery period or when lost and beyond aid would only make tough times incredibly worse. There isn't room for any degree of recklessness.

The need for caution would trickle down to the very simplest of activities. If you had to walk on rugged terrain, for instance, you might look for a good walking stick before pressing ahead. You should still step carefully all along the path. Turning an ankle on the common day is enough to create some pretty serious inconvenience. Driving might become difficult. You might need crutches. Turning an ankle in a survival situation that would require hiking and hard physical labor would minimally mean some pretty serious misery. It could ultimately lead to your demise.

You would have to keep a close eye out for anything sharp on the ground or otherwise. You should step with utmost care if in water and unable to see what's resting beneath. Those without access to medical care should complete their work methodically and with a good measure of patience. There isn't room for an accident. It really couldn't be considered an accident if you aren't taking appropriate precautions at a time in which it's so necessary.

Accounting for the potential lack of medical care through preparations is in another sense limiting the possibility you would need it. As discussed earlier, maintaining your health over the long term as a matter of lifestyle provides the best chances to survive and live comfortably at any time, and most notably, during any recovery period. The importance of decent strength and endurance can't be understated. Conversely, poor health could be hazardous should you lack access to your everyday means of managing your conditions.

Those who couldn't go for extended periods without trips to the doctor based on chronic conditions stand a greater chance of becoming a casualty of disaster. Statistics speak to the importance of physical ability and wellbeing. The very old and very young are the most frequent victims of any disaster.

The risk to those managing chronic issues would only increase should a disaster debilitate the community for any lengthy period of time. Prescriptions are tied to a particular pharmacy or pharmacy chain. If your relied upon drug store is closed up and you can't reach your doctor, you're out of luck.

Everyone should get certified in CPR. You could use what you learn to save someone's life.

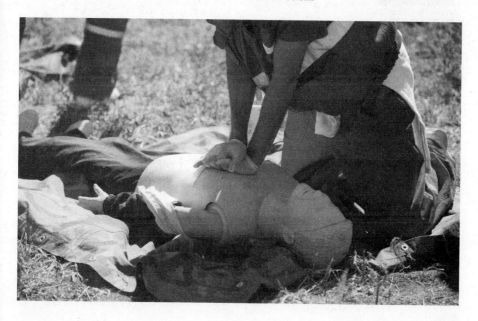

It's worth repeating: trips to the gym, evening jogs or even good brisk walks are part of your preparation efforts and deserve the same level of attention as building up food storage. Eating decent balanced meals instead of relying on greasy pizzas three nights each week is taking an effort toward preparedness just as is buying that new generator. Health takes work, though there's little in life that's worthwhile that doesn't require some degree of effort.

Even those who watch their diets and get their workouts in should keep on top of their health statuses. It makes a lot of sense to head into the doctor's office to get a physical on an annual basis. It would allow you to get some advice and quickly get a handle on any developing health issues before they grow more serious.

Preparation in its entirety is a practice of maintaining vigilance and there's no area in which it's more important than health. Our health is truly the most important thing we have. Preppers should act decisively and intentionally toward the ends of their wellbeing.

Doctors are smart people. It's worth following their advice. It's particularly true for all of those frequently repeated messages that too often fall on deaf ears. Put down the cigarettes. Avoid the fast food. Back away from the television screen and get active.

Those already struggling with some health conditions would want to keep their health at top of mind when working through a recovery. You should recognize your limits and make a point against taking unnecessary risks when at all possible. If the out-of-shape man with the heart problem doesn't have access to his doctor, he might be wiser in having his two in-shape sons provide some help if there's a heavy supply of water to haul home.

The medical side of prepping certainly isn't one of the easier pieces of the preparedness lifestyle. Maintaining health is a part of preparation that comes to play through any number of decisions every single day. Accounting for health in the wake of disaster further takes some thought in areas where most people just aren't comfortable spending it.

It is frightening to confront the possibility of injury or failing health. It's yet more difficult to consider encountering those difficulties without having a helping hand from within our skilled medical community. The best remedy to fear is always action.

Our lives have plenty to offer us. The one thing we'll never get from life is guarantees. Solid effort can make up a lot of the difference when circumstances strip a community of its comforts. Preparation recognizes we really do have the

CUSTOM FIRST AID KITS

You might not come to recognize the true value of a well-stocked, high-quality first aid kit until reaching a frightening moment in which it becomes a big-time necessity. Pre-packed kits in a variety of sizes and offerings are available at almost any store. The prepper would want to do a little better.

Most families have a first aid kit. The pre-assembled kits available at pharmacies and department stores generally provide what's needed to get through many trauma situations. Often, however, the goods packed inside aren't of the same quality you would find when buying items individually. Those who've long had these kits on hand might decide to build better versions from scratch.

It would start with a durable tote bag, a supply list and a trip to the nearby drug store. It would require some time and would certainly require some cash beyond the price tags on the ready-made versions sitting in the same store aisle. Some of the very basic kits out there go for $20 or less.

Those completely unprepared might start with a few of those basic kits. You could spend a little to make sure the home and vehicles are covered. You could then make adjustments when able. Having lesser quality items is better than having nothing ready. No one could predict just when that gear would become vital. Examine what's packed inside. If the bandages are poor, you could pick up some replacements during the next store visit. The same holds true for any of those contingencies.

Basic kits are precisely that. They'd include gauze, tape and bandages in a variety of sizes. They'll carry a few simple tools such as a tweezers and scissors. Any kit would have antibiotic and burn ointments. A pre-packed kit would have alcohol pads or other means to clean a wound.

A prepper would want to add to those kits in ways that meet specific family needs and the full capabilities you would want in an emergency situation. The basic kit isn't often going to have a reliable tourniquet. Many wouldn't include splints that would allow you to provide care for a bone break.

Those with severe allergies would stash away some EpiPens and medications of their choice. I suffer pretty severe headaches without a good influx of caffeine, and therefore I pack in some caffeine tablets into mine. Many people have preferences as it comes to painkillers.

Those who want a good, ready-made kit could go online and purchase a military Improved First Aid Kit. They're specifically made for battle trauma. The bandages, ointments, gauze, tape and other goods in an IFAK would come with higher quality than kits you would find at the store. They come with a tourniquet designed for combat that's easy to use.

The first step is to prepare. The next is to improve your preps. It's worth the effort to make sure the family is not only covered in terms of first aid but to the best extent possible in recognizing the potentially dangerous, high-stress situations during which these kits would come into play.

power to shift the balance to our favor at times of difficulty.

You could simply hope for the best. It wouldn't do much good. You could resign yourself to the idea that you lack the willpower to maintain a workout plan or are simply unable to handle the responsibility of administering first aid. In that case, you'd just as much resign yourself to plenty of worry when driving past the damaged pharmacy. A lack of effort now might later lead to a place in line, waiting with fear among scores of other injured people after the tornado levels the town.

Better yet, get to work now and be able to provide for yourself later. Should a painful, though non-life-threatening injury happen, you'd be able to rely on the skills, knowledge and confidence opened up through learning long before the emergency came to be. It all starts with attitude.

You would certainly choose a doctor and sterile treatment room if it were available. Similarly, you would want the simplicity and usual safety of the kitchen faucet during a water contamination emergency. Tough times are called such for a reason. Sometimes, an adequate solution will have to do if an otherwise preferable one just isn't there.

It's doable. People throughout history have done it all before.

Prepping is a practice that recognizes just how much we can accomplish with proper effort. You might think back to those encouraging words that each of us heard while growing up: "You can do anything if you put your mind to it."

Of course, it's not an objective fact. Only a select few, for instance, are going to start in centerfield for the Detroit Tigers. The country doesn't have millions of presidents or astronauts. Those words all the same offer some significant truth. All of us can indeed do far more than we think we're capable of with thought, a strong drive and all the work that comes along with it.

Preparedness is about taking charge. It's coming to recognize that we can take care of ourselves. It's a recognition that no good can come from simply ignoring the facts. Bad things happen. They happen frequently. They could happen to us. What, then, can we do about it?

We can make a good life for ourselves and families regardless of what Mother Nature throws into our paths. It's just a matter of thinking and following through to make sure our basic needs are covered for tomorrow just as they are for today. You can gain a lot of strength when coming to recognize just how much you can do on your own.

Building toward self-reliance is a

task that recognizes the community-at-large doesn't always have the best answers. We know and value ourselves and our families far more than anyone else. Getting to work on preparedness efforts recognizes the folly in simply hoping for handouts when emergency strikes. Anyone can do better. Even the best, most efficient aid offered after disaster — help that firmly accounts for the rule of threes — isn't bound to suit anyone's individual needs very well.

Know your meds and be mindful of your supply. If your relied upon drugstore is closed up and you can't reach your doctor, you could be out of luck.

A good life and a life of ease and comfort aren't always synonymous. Too many have been spellbound by our seemingly endless list of conveniences, whether it's gadgets and gizmos or quick access to businesses that provide every service under the sun. We can accomplish an awful lot by buckling down and getting to work. Many Americans have forgotten the ingenuity that incrementally built up and led to everything we have in this amazing modern era.

Prepping makes great sense for those who have the very best interests of their families in mind. It's a smart path to walk down. It's a path at the heart of what America really means.

Self-reliance isn't specifically written into our Bill of Rights, but you can find that way of life between the lines and throughout that critical document. It speaks to who we always were and what we were always about as a nation. It's the very definition of freedom. It's a matter of making our ways and meeting our needs as we individually see fit. It's a matter of getting the job done without waiting on someone else.

Our country was founded with the Declaration of Independence. We've quickly reached a place of unfortunate irony. We've reached a point in history where far too many are completely dependent on others to meet so many of their most basic needs. Many would be lost and struggling should all of that modern ease disappear. It could happen in minutes. It doesn't have to be that way.

It's worth stepping back and considering how life used to be. It's worth examining the attitudes and work ethics of our forefathers. It's worth remembering the great things that happened when people put their hands and minds to work. History is our best teacher.

This country we enjoy wouldn't be anything near what it is today if it wasn't for many great men and women — some recognized by history and others not — who took some big burdens on their shoulders. They recognized that, "If I don't do it, nobody else will." They made so many great things happen. Americans today are still afforded

the right to choose their own paths. You could choose the easy path and settle on reliance in others. You could put forth some more effort and choose the freedom of doing it your own way.

Emergency call centers are easily overwhelmed in a disaster. Take responsibility for your well-being and that of your family by being prepared for medical emergencies.

Take confidence as plans start to develop. Most of all, take comfort. Preparation takes some thought and some work but offers precisely that in the face of all the difficulties that are part of this turbulent world.

All of us have our minds and our hands. All of us can overcome a great deal more than many would ever figure. Just as generation after generation before us, we're still all very capable of doing so on our own terms.

Practice your first aid skills to increase your confidence.